P9-BJA-068

VITAL CHURCH MANAGEMENT

Philip M. Larson, Jr.

JOHN KNOX PRESS
ATLANTA

Credit is hereby given to *Church Management* magazine, now the *Clergy Journal.*

Library of Congress Cataloging in Publication Data

Larson, Philip M
  Vital church management.

  1. Church management. I. Title.
BV652.L35   254   76-12394
ISBN 0-8042-1883-8

Contents

Introduction

Religion is coming back to life in the seventies.

Since the mid-1950s the church has shown a decline in membership relative to population growth. During the sixties many churches closed.

To bring the church back to life in the days ahead we should all keep our eyes and ears open, and read everything we can in the field of parish administration.

Seminaries have often failed to prepare ministers for their daily work out in the field. Some seminaries have failed to offer up-dated courses in the field of Parish Administration. Clergy are schooled in homiletics and the Bible, but when they are put out in the field they tremble during their first funeral service; they come close to fainting on their first hospital call, and they shake during their first wedding ceremony. The first meeting with the governing board of a church can be traumatic. Some ministers are prepared only to give the opening prayer.

When we are assigned to our first church we sit in our study at home or in the church and wonder, "What should I do now?" Clergy who are criticized for not doing their work are generally those who do not know exactly what their work is. Those who are evangelists know they want to save souls, but the ministry requires much more today in most of our churches.

The health of the local church is not dependent upon the numbers of people saved or unsaved; it is dependent on how well the pastor knows how to relate his people happily to one another. The goal of religion in the Lord's Prayer is clear: "Thy kingdom come . . . on EARTH as it is in heaven." And the kingdom of peace and love and light will never come on earth unless clergy are trained in basic day-to-day parish administration.

Making the church come alive boils down to one word: WORK. If we do not know how to work, we are doomed to fail. We cannot speak in generalities. The work of the church is a very real occupation. Every minister and every church member must be encouraged to get down to the nitty-gritty. We must learn how to relate in the kingdom on earth.

1

Building a Job Outline
to Bring the Church Alive

Lay leaders should help their minister work out a job outline and the minister should seek advice from them.

The task of being a minister is difficult, extremely difficult. Church members often forget that they traditionally "call" their ministers. They do not "hire" them. They are "called" to serve as God and conscience dictate, not as others dictate. Granted, ministers should always be open to suggestions from their parishioners, but they alone, in the silence of their rooms, must choose priorities. No layperson could possibly understand the challenge of having so many choices as to how to spend one's time.

In order to give even a faint grasp of the magnitude of the problem, the following outline is set forth. It will be an asset to anyone in the ministry. Give a copy of the outline to your governing body and have *them* fill in the blanks. They will readily see that no minister could possibly do everything, and to do even the minimum amount of work required will take in excess of a forty-hour week or even a six-day week. The "priority" will indicate which of the many tasks is to be done first.

To use this sheet, the minister should mail it out to church leaders a week before meeting with them. At that time the total ministry of the church can be openly discussed and priorities agreed upon. Ministers should fill in their own sheets and bring them to the meeting to discuss their personal reasons for their priorities. Priorities do change. At one time finance may be a top priority for many church leaders, another time it will be membership or youth, depending on what tasks are presently being done so well that attention can be switched to new priorities.

This outline is to be used as a functional tool in aiding the minister to serve people better and to help the people understand the task of the minister. It should be presented to highlight the reasons for the minister's "call" and not used as a device to tell a pastor what to do as a "hired hand."

We can see from the outline that clergy face an impossible task, one which has caused many of us to fail and fall by the wayside without support from our people. It is also a task well worth doing that brings strength and courage and an indomitable spirit into the ministry. The ministry can strengthen us if the congregation applies itself to aiding the minister in his growth. Congregations can make the minister rather than vice versa. Bringing the church alive is a two way venture. Every minister learns from the church leadership as well as the church members learn from the minister.

In working on the construction of a job outline it should always be remembered that the married minister has a primary obligation to family. Ministers too often make the mistake of neglecting their family life for their calling and this can be destructive of the family, often leading to divorce and upheaval in their churches.

It is difficult to ascertain how the woman minister will share the responsibility of raising the family with her husband. We do not have enough data and feedback in this area at this time; but the investment of time, imagination, and love will surely be the same.

No church will be served well if the ministers' commitments to the church family exceed that which they give to their own families. Ministers, like other laypersons, should be available to their children on a daily basis. Family gatherings and vacation plans should be worked out cooperatively to the health and welfare of all. Just as the minister and his or her mate may need time away from their children to be alone, we also know that children too can grow during a vacation from their parents.

In short, when building a "job outline" keep your family in mind and structure time for them also.

JOB OUTLINE

Please fill in the blanks

I.   How many hours a week should the minister work? ____
     How many days a week should a minister work? ____
     How long should vacation be? ____

II. Which tasks of those mentioned below should be done first, second, third, etc.? Those with an asterisk are generally considered absolute musts. (This is only a partial listing.)

	Total Hours	Priority

1. *WORSHIP
Reading ___ Writing ___ Typing out ___
Choosing of hymns ___ Choice of readings ___
Printing of the order of worship, folding ___

2. PROGRAM
(Consulting, coordinating, advising, attending)
Beacon Club for couples and singles ___
Men's Club ___   Women's Alliance ___
Membership Nights ___ Finance Committee ___
Seminars ___   Youth Work ___
Church Bowling League ___ Other ___

3. COMMITTEE WORK (Planning, consulting, advising, coordinating, attending)
Governing Board ___   Religious Education ___
Membership ___   Finance Com. ___
Property Com. ___   Hospital Com. ___
Missions ___   Music Com. ___
Worship Com. ___   Social Action Com. ___
Other ___

4. *COUNSELING
Marriage ___   Premarital ___
Individual ___   Family ___
Non-members ___   Addicts ___
Suicides ___   Alcoholics ___
Criminal ___   Mentally ill ___
Other ___

5. *CALLING
Sick (hospital) ___   Backsliders ___
Shut-ins ___   Newcomers ___
Aged ___   Bereaved ___
Routine ___   Door knocking ___

6. *OFFICE WORK
Telephoning ___   Correspondence ___
Mimeographing ___   Filing, addressing,
Parish planning ___   and collating ___
Other ___

7. SOCIAL ACTION
Civil Rights ___   Protests ___
NAACP ___   PTA ___
Politics ___   Library ___
Ecology ___   Other ___

	Total Hours	Priority
8. PUBLIC RELATIONS Speaking Out, High School Students, PTAs, Service Clubs, Radio, TV, etc. _____ Membership in Service Clubs, Chamber of Commerce, YMCA, Mental Health Assoc. etc.____ Little League, Historical Society _____ Writing news, ads, and press releases _____ Other _____		
9. *MINISTERIAL FUNCTIONS (Including advising and time to perform) Weddings ____ Funerals ____ Baptisms or Christenings ____ Other ____		
10. DENOMINATIONAL AFFAIRS Local district concerns ____ National affiliation and meetings ____ Ministers Association ____		
11. PERSONAL GROWTH Meditation and reading ____ Writing ____ Taking instruction, classes, seminars ____ Attending local ministers meetings and discussions ____ Teaching ____ Other ____		
12. MISCELLANEOUS Receiving calls from non-members in home ____ Entertaining in the home ____ Accepting invitations to homes of parishioners____		
GRAND TOTAL OF WEEKLY HOURS		

Note: Monthly events can be divided by four for a weekly figure. *Remember*, any item left unfilled will have an impact on the ministry of the church. If any task is left undone, then a lay member must be ready to pick it up.

Ministers and church members often find themselves in a quandary as to how to bring their congregations to life. In every parish the work mounts. Committee meetings seem endless. Keeping track of numerous appointments seems impossible. Pastoral demands are ever pressing. The minister must have support from lay leaders.

The daily routine of a minister is hard to stabilize, but to be effective, the modern pastor and parish must learn to plan the workweek as carefully as any other professional. Our seminaries should instruct all students in the importance of planning their time. A suggested outline of how to plan a minister's workweek is outlined.

MONDAY MORNING 9–12 A.M. Study
1. Review the events of Sunday.
2. Review the weekly calendar of meetings and events.
3. Look over the complete mailing list and plan nine calls and three alternate calls for the week.
4. Choose your sermon topic for the next Sunday, and place reference materials on your desk.
5. Spend a few moments in self-assessment and meditation.
6. In-depth reading or study.

MONDAY AFTERNOON 1–4:30 P.M.
1. Make three scheduled calls.

TUESDAY   Day off

WEDNESDAY 9–12 A.M.,   1–5 P.M.,   7–9 P.M.
Spend Wednesday in your study.
1. Outline your sermon.
2. Prepare the Order of Service.
3. Dispose of all paper work and correspondence.
4. Prepare any newspaper publicity necessary.
5. Plan the content of the Sunday bulletin.
6. Make notations for the parish newsletter.
7. Do some reading in the field of Parish Administration to gain new insights in church growth.
8. Do some reading in pastoral psychology for counseling experiences.
9. Plan your committee meetings agenda for the month.
10. Keep Wednesday evenings open for counseling those who cannot be seen during the day.
11. If no counseling appointments are scheduled and the other day's tasks are completed, make two calls in the evening on two new families.

THURSDAY MORNING 9–12 A.M.
1. Mimeograph Sunday bulletins.
2. Call the newspapers or deliver material for publicity.
3. Telephone parishioners in relation to committee work, general consultation, or to inquire as to their health, etc.
4. Read and study in relation to preparation of sermon.

THURSDAY AFTERNOON 1–4:30 P.M.
1. Make three calls as planned.

FRIDAY MORNING 9–12 P.M.
1. Work out the details of your sermon and the illustrations, and do further reading for sermon preparation.

FRIDAY AFTERNOON 1–5:30 P.M.
1. Make calls as planned.

SATURDAY
1. Type out your sermon as you will deliver it, take it home and read
    it upon retiring.
2. Take Saturday afternoon and evening off so that you will be well
    rested for Sunday's routine.

Many ministers and laity upon reading this schedule will be critical
of arranging for only nine calls. Others will feel that to end the day
at 4:30 is too early. Some will question the feasibility of Tuesday as the
day off, when Monday is traditional. Some will note that night work is
not mentioned, and others will wonder about the advisability of spending all day Wednesday in the study.

A few words of explanation are in order.

Calling is always difficult to schedule and will be discussed in a later
chapter. Many ministers of larger churches call on the sick, the troubled, the elderly, and newcomers, and do not make time for average
church-going lay members because they can see them during the work
of the church. To limit one's calling simplifies the pastoral work and
focuses pastoral attention where it is most needed. It is best NOT to
plan too many calls, because sooner or later you will fall hopelessly
behind. When this happens, many ministers throw up their hands in
despair and tend to give up altogether. Their calling becomes "hit or
miss" and mostly "miss." If the calls that we do plan are important it
will take us more than a few moments to complete them. Some calls
may require two or three hours of our time. When this happens we see
the wisdom of underscheduling our calling and thus remaining free
from anxiety and frustration in not meeting our goals. There will be
times when scheduled calls move quickly and you might make more
than three calls in an afternoon, but this is rare. You will note that if
the above schedule is kept, at the end of the church year you will have
made a minimum of approximately 432 calls. This is an excellent
average to maintain and still do all the other things demanded of you.
The calling day ends at 4:30 for two reasons: (1) the average housewife
begins to prepare for her family's arrival at this time; (2) if you have
night meetings you should have some rest beforehand.

Tuesday was chosen as the day off because Monday should be spent
in retrospection and follow-up. By this it is meant that you should recall the events of Sunday morning. Who was conspicuously absent?
Who asked for a call at the door? Who requested that you consider a

specific matter? How did the sermon go over? Did the order of service run smoothly? If you put off these important considerations until Tuesday, your memory will be dimmed unless you have a church secretary taking notes at your side on Sunday morning. After you have considered the matters that arose on Sunday and followed through on them, you will be ready for a relaxed Tuesday off and free from any pressing concerns. You will feel that you have more than deserved a day off, and that nothing should rightly interfere with it.

Spending one full day in the office on Wednesday will keep you up-to-date in correspondence and paper work. Most ministers are noted for their poor handling of correspondence.

In the quiet of the study, with a full day ahead, ministers can scan their entire area of work and see it as a whole. Such a day is invaluable and an absolute necessity: a day of "finding one's self," of seeing the whole job, and knowing one's place in the scheme of the church. Time should also be spent in prayer and reflection.

In saving Wednesday night for evening counseling sessions, ministers can arrange to see husbands whom they have not been able to see during the daytime calls. Marriage counseling, premarital counseling, wedding rehearsals, and other such work can be arranged on Wednesday evening. The evening could be spent in study for counseling preparation.

One morning a week should be devoted to preparation and disbursement of news to the local newspapers. Too many churches receive very little publicity, not because the papers are not interested, but because the pastors do not take the time to present the material properly or to request special coverage of an event. All press releases should contain the five Ws: who, what, when, where, and why. Releases should be double-spaced and your phone number and name signed on each release.

We often neglect to use the telephone. Its use cannot be stressed strongly enough. It is an indispensable ally. When a member who attends church regularly is absent, a call of inquiry as to health shows concern. Committee chairmen often like a phone call reminding them of their committee work. A brief call of congratulations to a student making the honor roll, to someone who has received a job promotion, to a young couple who have announced their engagement, to the janitor for doing a good job in cleaning, to the local politician, to the police for exemplary duty, and to others who have helped your ministry. Telephoning can prove to be a great asset to the busy pastor.

Evenings are often taken up with meetings. If it is possible, schedule a certain number of your church committee meetings on the same night of the month at the church. You may then be able to consult easily with each committee by traveling from room to room. At the end of "Committee Night" you can all gather for worship and refreshments.

Many evenings should be spent in reading, especially biographies and the Bible, for by the renewal of your mind you will preach more easily and more effectively.

Decide each year just how many community activities you will serve and the evening time allotted to each. Do not overextend yourself in community affairs.

Some evenings will be given to "Membership Nights." By this is meant that newcomers will meet in a member's home by invitation for discussion with you and your spouse concerning the church.

If you have such nights, it will ease the evening calling burden because you can visit with many newcomers all on one night and they can get to know one another.

It is a good idea to choose your sermon subject on Monday because all during the week you can ponder your message, study Biblical texts, and consult reference material. On Wednesday you can outline it. On Friday detail it with illustrations. On Saturday morning you can complete the job and relax Saturday afternoon. Read your sermon over Saturday night and sleep on it. With proper planning, sermon writing will not be difficult, and you will be mentally ready to deliver the message on Sunday morning.

Ministers are professionals, not amateurs. Their lay leaders should be fully aware of their "job outline" and support it. Pastors should know their job well, schedule their time with as much precision as possible, and take time off to conserve mind and body so they can work without exhaustion and serve the Lord with gladness.

If church members fully understand the job outline they will be more sympathetic, helpful, and understanding. They should be involved in the nitty-gritty of bringing the church alive.

2
On Coming Alive Using the Principles of Business

When you enter a lawyer's office, you are probably overawed by the volume of books surrounding you on the subject of how to practice law. When we enter a doctor's office we may notice the many books relative to the practice of medicine. But when a layman enters the minister's study he would be hard pressed to find even one book on how to run a church!

Some seminaries are remiss. The field of parish administration has been neglected since the church began. Our young ministers entering their first church are not prepared to organize the parish for growth, and too often they fail. Young ministers usually start in a struggling, small, divided church, and last about three years, then leave with a great sigh of relief. The small church stays small because the minister doesn't know how to organize it, doesn't wish to form committees and groups, to "play politics," to do the mimeographing, the telephoning, and all the thinking and planning that goes with administrative leadership. The church people know that they are going to see a continual succession of pastors, all of whom change things at will and whim upon arrival. Thus the small churches become smaller or die altogether, and the larger churches, previously organized by someone who knew parish administration, get bigger.

Our city churches are dying for lack of leadership. One dying city church called me to talk with them about their plight. No sooner had I passed out material relative to publicity, public relations, membership and finance, than I overheard some older member say, "We don't want any of that Madison Avenue stuff."

When a church begins to die, it is generally because a clique of members over fifty years of age feels threatened by any new members. They have their own well established program at their age level and they don't see any need for Madison Avenue stuff, or for that matter any need for any new members who will change things. Thus a church dies; but the death is obvious only to a few of the older people who are young at heart and who are outgoing and sincerely interested in belonging to a vibrant, progressive church.

Diehards will always blame the minister for the demise of the church and seldom recognize their own thoughtless and self-centered ruts. In fact they will expound on their great sacrifices, saying, "If it weren't for us this church would close." It is often because of them that it closes! Unless a minister is called who knows how to meet the needs of the people and *at the same time* can organize the church school and can interest young couples in church involvement, it will close.

In order to preach, meet the needs of the elderly, and to organize the church for children and young adults, a minister must be well schooled in Madison Avenue stuff. We must be able to take a dying church and make it live again. It takes a good five to ten years and a strong dose of Madison Avenue stuff which really is not so bad tasting after all.

What is this Madison Avenue stuff? Simply this:

1. Making calls on the right people at the right time for the right purpose.
2. Emphasizing youth and church school programs.
3. Reorganization of all committees and delineation of the goals of each.
4. The perfection of the product (worship and preaching) for the atomic age.
5. The analysis of your image in the community.
6. The awareness of population mobility and what areas in your city will produce prospective members.
7. A planned program of church advertising and public relations (after the product is perfected, namely *church school* and *worship* service).
8. A well planned approach for the involvement of newcomers.
9. An open structure of church committees to add members at any time. There should be no closed meetings.
10. The starting of groups that cover all ages with persistence and imagination.

This is only a brief listing of Madison Avenue stuff. It is common sense for churches, but everyone knows common sense is uncommon. The dying city church and the struggling country church could use some of the common sense of the business world.

What is it that people on Madison Avenue know? They all know about the "Four Ps".

Almost every church has business people in it who want the church to be "run like a business." Yet most ministers have had little business experience.

Executives in industry have a three-stage decision problem:

1. To which of their many problems should they direct their attention?
2. How much time, effort, and expense should they invest in resolving the problem?
3. What solution will meet the problem best?

Organizing a church is similar to organizing a business in many respects and the above three questions are relevant to anyone's ministry.

The minister may be well aware of the problems in the church and should be able to establish priorities. It will then be the minister's job to convince the governing board to spend time, money, and effort relative to these priorities. The solution to the many problems should lie in a joint effort.

In business there are four main concerns: Product, Place, Price, and Promotion. These are the "Four Ps" of the business world:

PRODUCT

What are the products of religion? What are the products of your particular church? Are you selling salvation? Are you selling the gospel? Are you selling Sunday school? Are you selling fellowship? Are you selling intellectual stimulation, social action, youth, peace, love, freedom? Perhaps you are "selling" all of these things, but in which order?

Which product is most needed by your customers at a given time? If your community of believers is growing in faith and aware of the gospel, you may place the church school on the top of your priority list. If the church school is well organized, and there is dissension in your midst, fellowship may move to the top of the priority list.

Once you have established priorities decide which of these "products" you will perfect and "sell." You cannot sell a product until you perfect it.

PLACE

The location of any business is vital. Shopping centers locate where they are easily accessible to the largest number of people and they provide ample parking. The stores are well denoted by signs and outwardly attract customers. The clerks are trained to be cheerful to all who enter.

Certainly churches should be accessible, should provide parking, should be outwardly attractive, and should have ushers and greeters who welcome everyone. Building and grounds should show that the proprietors care about their assets. A poor location and no parking, coupled with an outwardly unattractive building will not attract customers, unless the product is matchless.

PROMOTION

People do not advertise a product until they feel it is good enough to sell. The preaching, the church school, the program should be at a constant level of performance.

Once the product is perfected, sell it! Use the news media and print brochures telling of your products. Organize a Publicity Committee to write press releases and keep the promotion constant.

The best promotion for any business is satisfied customers. When a church is divided and in a state of tension, new people will not be attracted—and if you have promoted fellowship no one will be fooled by your false advertising.

PRICE

What price will you put on your product? The price we pay for religion is ourselves. We must give of ourselves. We should request a fair price for our product. Some churches emphasize tithing, others "dues," most "pledges." Anything considered cheap is not held dearly. "Whosoever finds his life shall lose it, and whosoever loses his life for my sake shall find it."

Looking at the "Four Ps" shows a very simple analogy between business and church. This type of analogy is understood by people in your congregation who have experience in business. They will respond, "Now you're talking my language. You're alive in my realm."

3
The Facts of Life and Death for Your Church

Without knowing the facts, you can kill your church. Many church members and boards are unfamiliar with the facts. They cannot tell you the total amount of money it takes to run their church. They are unaware of how much money the congregation contributes in relation to endowment income. Others have no idea as to the number of active members or how many committees and groups are active. To deal with church problems, the membership must know the facts! Too often even ministers do not have accurate facts and this impairs their effectiveness.

To ascertain the lack of awareness of these facts mimeograph and distribute a "fact-sheet" to the governing board and then study the results. Such a sheet with areas for concern is found on the following page.

Your church board will enjoy digging into this fact-finding process. They will uncover a number of enlightening observations. They will come alive!

The interpretation of the above facts is important. Many boards will be surprised to know that the active membership is not what they expected it to be. If the active membership is smaller than surmised it will be obvious that the board really cannot expect a larger church attendance, especially when our Protestant churches generally average one-third of the membership at morning worship.

In listing the active groups it may be apparent that some age group or interest has been entirely neglected. Question eight indicates which age group is missing and why it is necessary to design a program for that particular age. It is amazing to find city churches near colleges with no active program for college students!

Questions five, six, and seven should indicate the adequacy of the Sunday school. A church will only grow as it enlists new young people

CHURCH FACT SHEET

1. Approximately what is the total active membership of
    our church?
2. What is the approximate average attendance at the
    Sunday morning service of worship?   __
3. List the church groups now active.   __

    _____
    _____
    _____
    _____

4. How many members approximately are NOT involved
    in any active group or committee work?   __
5. How many children are enrolled in the Sunday school?   __
6. How many teachers and staff people are involved in the
    work of the church school?   __
7. Are our Sunday school facilities adequate?   __
8. What age groups are missing in our church membership?
    Fill in the blanks and then draw a pyramid of our
    membership.
                    Number of Members
        Age 65 and over   _____
            50 to 65   _____
            40 to 49   _____
            30 to 39   _____
            20 to 29   _____
            11 to 19   _____
             1 to 11   _____
9. What is the present yearly operating expense?
10. What is the yearly total pledged and given?   __
                        and
    How many pledging units are there?
11. What is the average weekly pledge per giving unit?
12. What is the total amount of income received through
    endowment funds?   __
13. How many churches are there in the community?   __
14. What is the population of the community?   __
15. What is the total membership of the churches in the
    community?   __
16. What is the reputation of our church in the community?
    (good, bad, radical, conservative, social club, etc.)   __
17. Is our church in good physical condition?   __
18. Do we offer easy parking?   __
19. Where do the largest number of young married people
    reside?   __
20. How far away is this residential area from our church?   __
21. How well located is our church?
    (good, fair, poor)   __
22. What "good deeds" does our church perform for the
    the world and this community?   __

and their children. A church cannot grow unless it offers the best Sunday school situation possible. Growth is often dependent on your religious education program and the facilities available along with man and woman teaching power.

Question eight is vital. A healthy church will have the largest number of members in the lower age brackets. The smallest number proportionately will be in the upper age groups. A healthy church membership chart will draw out to a perfect pyramid. An upside down pyramid spells annihilation. An hourglass pyramid indicates that the church should concentrate on the middle-aged. Where the pyramid narrows, concentration on that age should be considered. When an age group is lacking, members should strive to create programs for that age group.

Older members' interests include women's sewing and charity, flower arranging, hospitality committee, luncheon groups, and a chess club. One Men's Club of older people was called THE PILLARS. All elderly members appreciate being asked their advice on all church issues.

Middle-aged interests include some of the above plus a particular niche where responsibility is clear. Ushering relates many to the church who would stay home unless actively involved. Committee work should include a large number of middle-agers. The middle-aged member does not want to be constantly put upon, but will gladly take a well-defined job. Committees should include Property, Ushering, Hospitality, Finance, Worship, Membership, Music, Publicity, Denominational Affairs, Missions, Sunday Greeters, Coffee Hour, Flowers, Transportation, and others mentioned in a later chapter.

Young couples and singles enjoy religious education and youth work, social action, couples' club activities designed primarily for fellowship, Church Fund raising projects, Parent Education courses, Sensitivity Training, Sports programs, Yoga, Interpretive Dance, Sunday Evening Seminars in homes, Diner's Club, Bridge Club, Theater Club, Meet with the Minister Nights, and all married couples want a good, cheerful, well-organized church Sunday school for their children.

Youth work should be divided into compatible age categories (19 years to 24; 15 years to 18; 11 years to 14). Youth work must offer a varied program decided upon by democratic procedure. The usual routine involves business, games, program, worship, and food, in that order, on a weekly schedule, and extracurricular events on a monthly basis.

Your church board may add a multitude of interests in order to build a healthy pyramid and good church growth.

Questions nine through twelve present the financial picture. The answers are self-explanatory. This picture can be greatly enlarged by breaking down the figures as to the number of pledges in any given financial category. Churches that are not raising enough money should examine whether or not the NEED for money is made obvious to the congregation; the needs should be defined clearly and made known blatantly. Money is only raised in relation to the obvious *needs* expressed.

Questions thirteen through sixteen are important in more than a subtle way. If there are ten churches in a community of ten thousand and the population evenly divided, each church has a potential of only one thousand members including children. If the population is composed of one-third of one particular faith then the odds are cut considerably. If your community has 60% Roman Catholics, and 5% Jews, your chances for growth are obviously limited. If only 48% of all Americans attend church that data should also be considered. Upon closer inspection we might learn that the "potential" is limited more by assumptions regarding race or culture than was realized. When church boards constantly mutter about church "growth" and why the minister doesn't do something about it they should check their facts. The facts might indicate that even the Apostle Paul would find it impossible to build up the church in that community. If the church has a poor reputation, church growth is hampered to a greater degree. In smaller communities the citizens know if a church is divided against itself, newcomers will avoid such an organization. If the church caters to the wealthy, church growth is thereby limited. If the church has a reputation as a "social" club," church growth is proportionately limited. A church board should have all the facts clearly in hand before jumping to conclusions about church growth.

Question seventeen is obvious because a passerby will judge the people in the church by how the church looks outside. Just as passersby judge us by our homes and the yards we keep. If we have a messy home we are considered messy people. People still judge books by their covers.

Question eighteen looms more and more important because parking problems are uppermost in people's minds. If we expect church growth we should offer easy parking. Churches could well take a tip from the new shopping centers and the huge parking areas necessary for a healthy business.

Questions nineteen, twenty, and twenty-one will often give the answer to why there is a lack of young couples. Our young people are moving to the suburbs. Statistics indicate that the average person will not consistently drive more than two miles to church. If the young couples all live over two miles from your church and your church offers poor facilities for religious education you should consider the possibility of moving. This fact added to the data from questions five, eight, thirteen, seventeen, and eighteen can indicate the need for relocation of your church.

The last question asks how well your church serves the community at home and abroad. A church should reach out to everyone possible. A live church shows a real concern for all people regardless of race, creed, or color.

There are many ways of pinpointing your church's problems. The process is slow because it is a constant one of reevaluation and factfinding. This process, however, can save your church from all kinds of frustrations and disagreements and should take place twice yearly.

All lay leaders should know the life-and-death facts and be able to decide where to put their time, energy, and money. To make the church come alive, know all the facts!

4
Building Life into Your Program

In early America the church was the center of all community life.

Those of us who are committed to the work of the church must develop a church program that serves the needs of every age and interest and return the church to the center of our community life.

We are all aware that we have a Bible to guide us. This fact is taken for granted.

We are also aware of the importance of preaching. Some ministers have perfected their art. They can publicly announce their appearance and spend thousands of dollars "selling" their message of salvation. Salvation after death is vital, but salvation on earth is also vital.

The views of Jesus regarded as the basic ethics in his preaching are:

"Walk the second mile."

"Turn the other cheek."

"Love your neighbor as yourself."

"Forgive seventy times seven."

"Do unto others that which you would have them do unto you."

"Of him who has much shall much be required."

"The greatest among you shall be the servant of all."

"Thy kindgom come . . . on earth as it is in heaven."

The "kingdom" will not come on earth without a hard-working, alive church dedicated to the basic ethics of the Sermon on the Mount. We must build churches filled with people who know how to relate religiously in many diverse ways, who come alive with the practice of religious ethics in the here and now.

For too long the church has not stressed its task of building peace in the here and now. In the sixties the social action movement was sometimes extremely radical and misguided. The religious activities of the sixties talked of "love"; yet the persons involved were incapable of showing that love in their own marriages, friendships, politics, and churches. They did not follow the teachings of the Sermon on the Mount.

To build a church takes work. It takes service. It takes sacrifice. It takes practical knowledge.

In chapter 2 I implied that we must relate to people where they are. I asserted that you cannot "sell a product until you perfect it." Some of us may be gifted by God to preach, and preach alone, and that is a tremendous gift to mankind, but others of us have to struggle with the day-to-day, nitty-gritty problems of the church and its people in the "field."

We need practical knowledge.

Chapter 3 helped us to gain practical facts to guide us in the use of our God-given energies. This chapter deals with more facts and a few ideas to inspire us to take wings and "soar like eagles" to come alive with new concepts that relate us happily in our church.

There is an infinite variety of ways to unite church members in fellowship and service.

The following is a brief list of ideas that may prove stimulating in our quest to build a strong church family:

1. The Sunday family dinner.
2. The church committee night.
3. The Sunday evening seminar.
4. The before-church coffee hour.
5. The meet with the minister night.
6. Biblical help for shut-ins.
7. Youth appointments for conversation.
8. A hymn-a-month.
9. The special-gifts notices.
10. The church council and yearly planning.
11. Youth work.
12. The top ten outdoor games for youth.
13. The top ten indoor games for youth.
14. Sensitivity training and small groups.
15. Couples and singles clubs.

An inventory of numerous ideas closes this chapter. Print the inventory, add or subtract to it, but make sure your church leadership is involved in the process.

THE SUNDAY DINNER AFTER WORSHIP

Many of our churches have planned a breakfast before morning worship, but few have staged an after-church dinner for the entire family and congregation. People are always happily related to one another when they eat together. The Sunday dinner should immediately follow the service. It should be a catered dinner so that no one has to work and all members can sit down leisurely together. The expenses can be paid entirely by the church, by reservation, or partially by the church and partially by a freewill offering. Such a Sunday family dinner is a truly unifying force, a cheerful occasion for all, and the church is sure to come alive with a spirit of "communion."

COMMITTEE FELLOWSHIP

Many churches are dying from a lack of good Christian fellowship. The congregation may be large or small but the people really may not know one another. They may not work well tegether, or jealousy and divisions of power may tend to weaken the church. Small groups are vital to keep a church alive, but occasions arise when everyone should unite in fellowship.

One way of integrating the membership is through the establishment of a monthly "Committee Fellowship Night." Each month all of your committees should gather together at the church. The evening would follow this plan:

Dinner	6:30- 7:30
Committee Meetings	8:00-10:00
Chairmen's Reports	10:00-10:20
Worship	10:20-10:35

Dinner

A catered dinner should be served to all committee members. The disciples probably ate together every evening, and church members would do well to eat together often in that example and spirit. Members may wear name tags or other methods may be devised for encouraging introductions. Having a catered dinner releases all members from kitchen work and the expense can be made up by passing the hat or from the church treasury if your church can afford it. The fellowship is worth the expense. If a dinner is not feasible, coffee and dessert can be served by an appointed committee.

The Committee Meeting

After the dinner the committees disperse to delegated rooms or areas to carry on their usual work. The minister, and staff, if such exists, should be available for consultation. The availability of the other committees affords an opportunity to compare notes on conflicting dates of planned events, arrange alliances of committees that might share some programs together, and ask other committee members' advice in specialized areas as needed.

The Chairman Reports

At the specified time the chairmen or secretaries of the various committees will read their minutes to the assembled body. The reports help to educate all assembled to the entire field of work encompassed by their church. Members will be encouraged to make proper suggestions to the chairmen of the committees and thus a large number of people become well informed of the total church program.

The Worship Service

The service of worship should not be longer than fifteen minutes. It serves to unite all to the greater cause of the church and to God. Such a service may be conducted by the committee members themselves and is a fitting ending to a night of work and fellowship.

During a "Committee Fellowship Night" many new ideas may blossom forth.

Some members may request that husbands or wives of committee members be welcomed to the dinner and that a program be arranged for them following the meal. One method of solving this problem is to compose your committees of husbands and wives where advisable.

Some members may wish to have their committees adjourn to a home from 8–10 P.M. and return for the reports and worship. This could be arranged when some members cannot arrive in time for the scheduled dinner.

Some churches may wish to have the worship service at a different hour and extend an open invitation to the entire church membership. Other churches may wish to call the evening "Family and Committee Night" and open the supper, report, and worship service to all in the church and offer a program for non-committee members from 8–10 P.M.

The "Committee Fellowship Night" and its routine may vary, and many innovations take place according to the people's wishes involved. The purpose remains the same, to help the church become more vital.

THE SUNDAY EVENING SEMINAR

In some suburban communities the evening prayer meeting is being replaced with a seminar. With the emphasis on education today, many of our younger people crave some intellectual stimulation, especially in the growth of their religious faith. Seminars are meetings at which church members present their views on religious subjects and all present discuss the area of concern. A panel approach involving parishioners is most common, but a speaker may present the subject for general discussion, or the minister might introduce the topic and keep the discussion alive. Seminars of this nature are most successful when held in HOMES of parishioners. The home adds warmth and freedom to the give-and-take of discussion and lends itself to an informal get-together. Some may wish to consider serving wine and cheese at the beginning and/or coffee and dessert at the conclusion. Seminar topics may range from religious education to death and immortality; from world religions to local religions; from politics to Bible; from women's liberation to modern philosophy. Members will learn to know one another better and to relate themselves to each other happily and creatively in the Sunday evening seminar.

THE COFFEE HOUR

The Sunday morning coffee hour will never replace the communion service, but it has often been called a type of modern "communion." The fellowship of the coffee hour is unifying. The after-church coffee hour has become a fad everywhere in America, but few churches have tried the *before*-church coffee hour. Such an "hour" is often more effective for religious purposes as it serves to set a mood of fellowship before people enter a worship service. The mother with young children often comes harried and physically and mentally depleted by the chore of getting her family ready. The before-church coffee hour offers her an opportunity to sit and relax and prepare herself for meditation in a way that no other activity might. Hosts and hostesses of the occasion see to it that those who attend are dispatched promptly for worship. Children meet early in a group for an assembly, for worship, or for classes; and nursery attendants must be available. The before-church coffee hour can be an encouraging factor in church attendance.

THE MEET WITH THE MINISTER NIGHT

A pleasant way to greet newcomers into the life of the church is to invite them to the homes of members. The invitation is a written note which invites the new person to the home for dessert and informal discussion with the minister and his or her spouse. The personal note is followed by a phone call the day before the gathering to add a personal touch and to get a final tally of the number of people to expect. The host and hostess are supported in their role as greeters by one or two other couples who are good church members. The minister leads the discussion in the area of the church, its programs and religious concepts.

Such evenings alleviate the stress of evening calls on the minister. One night so arranged makes it possible for the minister to see four or more couples at once and also to give these couples an opportunity to make friends with other church-related couples.

A monthly "Meet with the Minister Night" can be successful beyond all expectations since newcomers so involved feel much freer about joining the church at a later date.

BIBLICAL HELP FOR SHUT-INS

The shut-in often needs a great deal of attention. Many of the elderly have served the church well and deserve as much attention as possible. One way of keeping them related to the church on a weekly basis is the mailing of Bible passages. The Bible book, chapter, and verse are listed. The shut-in can then look up the quotation and ponder its meaning. Each passage should be specially chosen for the individual shut-in—in relation to the circumstances that person faces. In a sense this is "bibliotherapy" and healthy non-directive counseling. Postcards may be mimeographed in advance leaving blank spaces for the book, chapter, and verse. They should have a brief salutation and the name of the church, signed personally by the minister. Busy pastors attempt to keep up on their calling, but often find it useful to appoint "Parish Visitors" to support this program.

YOUTH APPOINTMENTS FOR CONVERSATION

Young people should occasionally have a real face-to-face confrontation with their ministers. In order to arrange such dialogue the minister may schedule hourly after-school appointments with every junior and senior high school student. This is a time-consuming task but well worth the effort. The purpose can be set forth in a letter to both parents and young people asserting that the minister would like to speak with the young person about his or her church, religion, and future plans. The purpose is to get to know one another better. Such conferences open the door to marriage counseling at a later date, or to immediate problems which the young person may need some help in facing. A chart of *all* appointments can be mailed to each family involved and posted on the church bulletin board, thus everyone is aware that all young people are involved and that this is a routine confrontation in your church. Some young people will not respond, but those who do will enjoy the pastoral relationship and concern more than can be measured.

THE HYMN-A-MONTH

Some congregations enjoy singing the same hymns over and over while others would like to sing new hymns. To introduce a new hymn, encourage the choir to learn it well and then announce that the new hymn will be the "hymn of the month." Each Sunday for an entire month the new hymn can be sung. By the end of the month it will be known well enough to be added to the list of old favorites.

THE SPECIAL-GIFTS NOTICES

There are times when funds are not available for specific needs: communion ware, office machines, Sunday school visual aids, and other items not included in the church budget. However, there are members of the church who would contribute to a specific need if they were aware of it. Such needs should be published on a bimonthly basis in the newsletter. The desired item, the need for it, the exact purchase price, and the place it might be purchased are important. The same needs should not be repeated over and over; an object asked for again and again may indicate that no one really feels it is needed or else someone would have purchased it. Funds are given toward church needs only to the degree that the need has been set forth clearly and understood. Notices asking for special-gifts should be a routine thing, objective and open, without laboring the issue. Keeping the congregation informed on the needs of the church discreetly, openly, and without anxiety can bring surprising results.

THE CHURCH COUNCIL AND THE YEARLY PLANNING

Planning an entire church program for the year looms as an impossible task. It is not. During June all committee chairmen and group leaders may gather as a "Church Council." Each leader and each chairman should come with notes regarding the day or night of the month they will meet and with some idea of their extracurricular activities. With this data before the Council, church events can be dated without conflicts of time and interests. Once the dates are established the routine functions of all committees and groups are delineated. It is amazing to find out how easily groups can schedule various events which are yearly occurrences. Committees may even set the place of meeting, if in homes, along with the date and the probable agenda. Such planning is in no wise impossible, and it is planning that makes an excellent church program where all are happily involved in service and worship.

As is said in Scouting, "planning makes it possible." Do try to plan your church year in June so that the fall opens with a well publicized start and the church "comes alive."

YOUTH

Youth work begins in the church school. It must continue with a Junior High Youth Group and a High School Youth Group.

Congenial advisers are the prerequisites.

The successful pattern of operation has not changed for decades except during the sixties, but even then it was only a matter of emphasis.

The pattern:

1. Arrival in an appropriate church room and being greeted by advisers.
2. Mixing games (outlined later).
3. Business meeting.
4. Program.
5. Worship.
6. Food and more games.

You will find this continued plan quite successful.

Junior High Youth should meet from 4 to 6 P.M., Sunday evenings.

High School Youth should meet from 6:30 to 8:30 P.M. on the evening of their choice, generally Sundays.

These time schedules are joyfully accepted by parents who need the rest from children at precisely these hours.

If possible, advisers should request the parents to bring the youth to the church, and if necessary, the advisers will provide transportation home. Normally, however, the advisers should not be expected to take youth home from church activities.

The extracurricular activities are too numerous to mention and the youth can offer innumerable suggestions for trips, overnights, charity, and church work.

Programs involve discussion, films, filmstrips, speakers from police, school, colleges, service organizations, radio announcers, hypnotists, magicians, and other professionals.

Too many churches lose their teenagers. The one way to keep them actively related to the church is with a vital youth program covering a multitude of needs and activities.

Following is a section on games which may be useful in the youth program (and other groups). However, be aware of the mood of the group—playing games does not go across well in all groups and this should be taken into consideration.

The Top Ten Outdoor Games for Youth

1. Steal the Bacon	6. Spud Ball
2. Crows and Cranes	7. Tug o' War
3. Pom-Pom	8. Wheelbarrow Race
4. Chicken Fight	9. Skin the Cat
5. Horse and Rider	10. Kickball

1. Steal the Bacon

Players choose two teams. Each team player has a number, from one on. They stand opposite each other about twenty yards apart. (Can be played inside if area is deemed large enough.)

The "bacon" is generally a knotted dish towel or neckerchief and is placed halfway between each team. The group leader will call a number and the player on each team who has that number will run out to bring home the "bacon." The object of the game is twofold: to steal the bacon by bringing it out of the center of the game area back home to your team, or to tag the opponent who tries to steal the bacon. In one sense a team is offensive minded while the other team may be defensive minded. Both teams stay at their lines unless more than one number is called. Only the numbers called go forth to steal the bacon, or to prevent the other team from stealing the bacon.

The team that gets the bacon back home without being tagged gets a point. If tagged, the other team gets a point. Fifteen points wins the game.

Example:

Number "One" is called by leader. A1 goes to defend from steal. B1 tries to maneuver to steal thinking he is faster runner. If a standoff occurs then a second or third number is called or even "All."

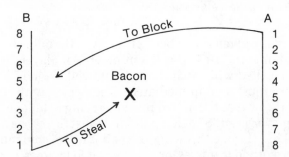

As in all games, players become boisterous, and rules on pushing or not pushing, proper use of hands, or no hands, must be made by the leader. With experience, players become adept at this game.

2. Crows and Cranes

Players choose two teams and line up within an *arm's length* of each other. Each team has a goal line, some ten yards behind them. One team is named "Crows," the other "Cranes." The leader will call either team name and the team called must run back quickly to their goal line without being touched by the opposite team who pursues. Any player tagged is out, and the team with one player left wins; or the game can end with any majority. Players who get tagged "out" do not like to sit too long on the sidelines.

3. Pom-Pom

All players stand on one side of the playing field and one of them is chosen for the center of the field. That one is "it." When "it" calls "Pom-Pom" all players must run across the field to the opposite goal line. "It" will try to tag them. Anyone tagged joins "it" in the center. Players run back and forth at the call of "Pom-Pom" until everyone is caught, or until those left are pronounced winners.

4. Chicken Fight

Here is a very simple game that can be used with all groups in all places to wile away the time. Players hold one foot up with their hands and HOP. While hopping they bump one another or dodge and feint, until all have fallen except the winner.

5. Horse and Rider

The larger players choose smaller ones who mount them piggyback. On a signal from the leader, horses with their riders bump one another until the horse and rider left standing wins. Riders may also pull other riders from their horses, thereby putting that team out. Girls like this game as much as boys do. If this version seems too rough, then horses and riders can run a relay race.

6. Spud Ball

All players are given a number. "It" is given the ball. "It" will throw the ball high into the air and call a number. All players will scatter. The number called will catch the ball and yell, "Spud," at which all other players must stop immediately. The person with the ball will then roll or throw it at the halted players, trying to hit one. If a player is hit, that player is an "S" of a "spud" and must throw the ball up; or if no player is hit, the one throwing the ball is an "S" and must throw it up. A player with four misses, or a player hit four times, or any combination of hits and misses is out.

7. Tug o' War

This is fun with the boys against the girls—and Junior High girls often win. Get a long rope, draw a line between the two teams, and then yell, "Pull."

8. *Wheelbarrow Race*

Each player picks a partner. One partner picks up the other's legs at the knees, while his partner is standing on his hands. At a signal the race is on and teamwork wins.

9. *Skin the Cat*

Players will choose two teams. The teams will line up, one player behind the other, with legs wide apart. The smallest players will be at the back of the line. The first player facing front will put his LEFT hand back through his legs and it will be grasped by the RIGHT hand of the player behind him and so on. At a signal, the smallest player in back will CREEP through the legs of the player in front, holding hands tight, and so on until the "cat is skinned," and the last player is first, and the first is last, all still holding hands.

10. *Kickball*

This game is played like baseball, only the ball is kicked after being rolled, and the bases are run. Players may be thrown out at bases, or be thrown out by being hit by a thrown ball. Use a light, big ball for quick outs and fast turns at "bat."

Imaginative leaders can devise many variations of some of these games in relation to the size and ability of the participants.

This is a good list of games to keep handy if you are a scout leader, a church youth group adviser, a teacher, or a camp counselor.

Help the kids to play their way to health!

The Top Ten Indoor Games for Youth

1. Picture Charades	6. Spin the Tin
2. Wink	7. Buzz Seven
3. Numbered Chairs	8. Rhythm Categories
4. Hot Potato	9. Drawing Portraits
5. Circle Number Bluff	10. What Would You Do If?

These games are for mixed groups, large or small; they need little equipment, and in most cases none at all. They are listed in the order of their popularity, at least, as I have found, after twenty years of working with children between the ages of 9 to 14.

1. *Picture Charades*

Two blackboards are required or several large sheets of paper. Chalk or crayons and pencils.

Choose two teams. The group leader will take a seat across the room with a paper and pencil in hand. At the leader's signal, a player from each team, by turn, will run to the chair, read a word on the leader's paper, then run back to the blackboard and draw the word. His teammates will try to guess the word from the drawing alone. No talking! No gestures! When the word is guessed, the player will run and touch the leader, and score one point. The EXACT word must be guessed, singular or plural, verb or noun. The team getting fifteen points first wins the game.

This game is a good adjunct to teaching lessons. A nature class will be given words from the lesson; a Bible class, a history class, etc.

Over the years, no game has been more popular than this one!

2. Wink

A mixed group is necessary for this circle game. Place the chairs in a circle and seat the girls. The boys take their places behind the girls. One chair is left empty, with a boy standing behind it. He will be "it," and will wink at any girl seated. The girl will jump up and run to the winker's chair, while the boy behind her will try to stop her by placing his hands upon her shoulders.

The boy whose chair is then empty is "it," and he will try to get another girl to escape. After five minutes, the boys will sit and the girls will stand behind them and try to prevent their escape to the winker.

3. Numbered Chairs

This is a game for any group, mixed or not, under twenty in number. (If the group is more than twenty, two games may be played at once with resulting anxiety, confusion, and fun.)

Chairs will be placed in a circle for the players and each chair will be numbered in turn from one to twenty (or whatever the number of players present). The chairs are numbered, NOT the players. Player in chair number one will call any number present; that player will *immediately* respond by calling another number. The group leader must decide if the response is wrong or too slow. Any player who fails must go to the highest numbered chair, while all other players move one numbered chair in the direction of that which was just vacated and take their new number. The object of the game is to move into the number one chair.

4. Hot Potato

This is a more active game for any type group. Players place their chairs in a circle. The player who is "it" will stand in the center of the circle. The "potato" can be a knotted dish towel, or some object that when passed will not injure the players. The players, because the "potato" is *hot* must pass it quickly across the circle, while "it" will try to intercept the "potato." If "it" intercepts the passed potato he takes the place of the player who threw it, who is then "it."

5. Circle Number Bluff

Any number of players can play. They will sit in a circle and each *player* will have a number that he will keep throughout the game. "It" will be blindfolded and will stand in the center of the circle, which should be as small as possible. "It" will call out two numbers. The numbers called must *immediately* rise and try to change places while "it," blindfolded swoops his arms to touch one of them. If a moving player is touched he is "it." In larger groups there can be two "its," and they can each call two numbers, or each may call three or more numbers, as the group leader decides.

6. Spin the Tin

Players will be seated in a circle and each player will be numbered. A tin cover or pie tin, or a similar flat tin dish may be used. "It" will take his or her place *anywhere* within the circle of players, spin the tin on its edge, and call out a number. The player whose number is called must catch the tin before it falls flat. If he does not, he or she is "it." When players become adept at this game, "it" may call out two numbers and they must scramble to catch the tin.

7. Buzz Seven

Players will be seated in a circle. The first player will call out number "one" and the player on the left will call number "two" and so on from left to right around the circle, but when a player comes to number SEVEN, or any number with a SEVEN in it, or a multiple of SEVEN that player must call out "BUZZ." If a player misses, he or she is out of the game. "Buzz" must be called out by a player at 7, 14, 17, 21, etc. The last two players remaining, win the game.

8. Rhythm Categories

Players will be seated in a circle and by vote of hands choose a "category." Categories most often chosen are: cars, cigarettes, cities, countries, trees, flowers, etc. Any category may be used.

The leader will direct the "rhythm" by slapping his knees twice, slapping his hands twice, and snapping his fingers twice. On the snap of the fingers the particular object of the category is mentioned. When every player has the rhythm, the leader will begin, and players will call out DIFFERENT objects within the category in rotation. When players lose the rhythm, they automatically drop out of the circle. Also, if players fail to name an object within the category, not already named, they are out. The last player left wins the game.

9. *Drawing Portraits*

Players will be seated around a table or on the floor. Each player must have paper and a pencil. When ready, all players will be asked to fold the paper in such a way that three sections will appear between the folds, as you would fold a letter for a long envelope. The player opens up the sheet and on the top portion draws the top of a person's head, and then folds the paper *back* so that the picture is not seen. At a call from the leader, the papers are passed on and each player draws the eyes, ears, and nose, and again folds the sheet back and passes it on. Players then draw the mouth and chin and neck and collar on the third section, then hold the paper until the signal is given to look at the creation, or portrait. Some very funny portraits can emerge from the players' imaginations.

10. *What Would You Do If?*

This is another imagination game. Each player sits around a table or on the floor with paper and pencil. The papers must be numbered and written upon before the game begins. The first player will put a number one on the top of his sheet and print across the top of the paper the words, "What would you do if . . ." The second player will also put a number one on top of his page and write the words, "I would . . ." across the top of the sheet. For every numbered 'What would you do if . . ." there must be a number to correspond, with the words "I would . . ." written at the top.

Each player, depending upon the title across the sheet, will finish the sentence, *not knowing* what his or her counterpart has written. Sheets are then passed around and number one reads: "What would you do if a monster ate this group?" or some such silly assertion; and then number two sheet is read: "I would jump in the lake." When no one knows what anyone else is writing, or replying, the game can be quite exciting.

Sensitivity Training and Small Groups

There are many ministers who have been well trained in the field of psychology and group interaction.

Some ministers feel that the only salvation for the church and for mankind is to teach people how to relate in small groups.

The rising divorce rate still suggests the need for small group interaction and for opportunities for increased knowledge about human emotions and relationships. While personal judgment is necessary, the insights that you learn in a small group may be applied in your relationships with family, friends, and co-workers.

As the church grows we cannot avoid splintering into men's groups, women's groups, couples and singles clubs, youth groups, sewing groups, choirs, youth groups, parent education groups, religious education groups, ad infinitum.

The "modern minister" must develop expertise in dealing with small groups.

SENSITIVITY TRAINING

The new fad called "Sensitivity Training" reached a peak during the early seventies, yet many ministers are just now trying to assess the efficacy of such experimentation.

Occasionally someone will call the movement "dangerous." They call it so quoting the old adage: *A little knowledge is a dangerous thing.* No knowledge is even more dangerous. The "dangers" of sensitivity training sessions has been placed at approximately .06.

The church has long dabbled in sensitivity training.

For centuries the church has served to build meaningful relationships and was in some respects the forerunner of GROUP THERAPY.

Frances Trollope writing about Cincinnati in 1832 says:

> When the room is full, the company of whom a vast majority are always women, are invited, entreated, and coaxed to confess before their brothers and sisters all their thoughts, faults, and follies. These confessions are strange scenes; the more they confess, the more invariably are they encouraged and caressed.

One could readily compare the old revival meetings with modern group therapy at Esalen or any other such meeting place where people gather for marathon sensitivity sessions.

The modern trend toward religious revival offers a great outlet for the expression of one's innermost feelings.

At the turn of the century Dr. Elwood Worcester of Emmanuel Church in Boston began special classes for those afflicted with TB. Modern group therapy classes are often composed of homogenous groupings of persons with ulcers, asthma, allergies, cancer.

The classes of Dr. Worcester eventually led to the Emmanuel Church Movement of health classes and was aided by Dr. Samuel McComb and one of America's first psychoanalysts, Dr. Isadore Coriat. The movement in early 1908 was criticized by an editorial in the journal of the New York Medical Society.

> The Emmanuel Church Movement in Boston which has resulted in establishing a clinic for the treatment of functional nervous and mental disorders, under the directorship of an able pastor, Dr. Worcester, has assumed such serious proportions and has been widely exploited . . .

It is interesting to note that the Christian Science Movement also began in Boston.

Meaningful relationships in religion were to lead one to both physical and mental health. Within the church people did confront, encounter, touch, express feelings, and relate with sensitivity.

Church boards and committees offered open discussion and free association and encouraged long standing friendships that are only witnessed in these times among older members. The "sewing circle" was a tremendous place for sensitivity training and the women of the church often shared deeper friendships than the men.

Ministers should experiment with new forms and new groups in an effort to bring about deeper relationships among their church members. The kingdom of heaven certainly will not be composed of strangers.

Occasionally young people seeking friendship will assert, "Only old people know how to be real friends." This is indeed tragic.

The word "sensitivity" became popular in the sixties but almost any other designation can be used by the imaginative minister. He may call his newly forming group, "Encounter Group," "Marriage Enrichment Group," "The Disciples," "Confrontation Group," "Fellowship Group." The name still has an attraction but the goal is always the same, namely the building of a beloved community.

Moreover, for our purposes we shall call the newly formed group a "Sensitivity Group."

Sensitivity training is not "Encounter" with primary emphasis on body contact.

Sensitivity training is not a "T-Group" with primary emphasis on solving a specific problem.

Sensitivity training is not "group therapy" where the emphasis is on catharsis, true confessions, etc.

Sensitivity training is not a cocktail party where emphasis is on sociability, drinking, small talk.

Sensitivity training is not a game, although games are usefully and consciously employed.

Sensitivity training is designed to bring "normal" people together in a relaxed setting for the purpose of learning how to put present feelings into words. The purpose of the training is growth.

Young adults are seeking frantically for meaningful relationships, and they will once again turn to the church as in the past. The "sensitivity group" may be a vital form of ministry for these people, and small groups can serve to make the church a dynamic place to be.

The setting for groups is designed to facilitate communication.

When one person "feels" what another person "feels" the communication has been successful. This empathy can be shown by verbal or non-verbal expression such as a pat on the back, the shaking of hands, the moving closer to the other person in the group circle. Embracing, kissing, hugging is in the realm of encounter and is generally discouraged, unless between husband and wife.

The result of any sensitivity is seen in the support of one group member for another. This empathy may carry itself beyond the boundary of the group into other human relations in order to develop in-depth relationships.

When healthy relationships develop they are enduring. This is to be distinguished between an affair, a flirtation, an infatuation, and similar rather fickle and short-lived liaisons. When sensitivity training leads to mutual support it lends itself to the religious goal of building the beloved community, or the "kingdom on earth." The mature person can establish in-depth, lasting relationships that are healthy for all and injure none.

This, of course, is the *ideal*. An *ideal* takes *work*. People who are not willing to work should not involve themselves in sensitivity training.

The role of the leader of a sensitivity group is to stimulate verbal confrontation. The verbal confrontation may be abusive and may lead to open conflict and such verbal combat should not be discouraged but "worked through." The leader must be knowledgeable, perceptive, and emphatic enough to stop confrontation at the point where the anxiety level is too high for one of the group members.

The trainer of the group reserves the right to make interpretation of verbal content and to lead the group process in a "directive" as well as a "non-directive" way. The trainer has the right to inject his own personal feelings and to have them accepted or rejected by group members.

When a group member, or the trainer, uncovers a behavioral pattern it should be discussed. If the person whose pattern is uncovered agrees with the interpretation then that person will be expected to work at changing the pattern within the group process as best he or she can, and as long as willing.

Members of a sensitivity group should be realistic in their expectations. All group sessions cannot be termed "successful" by every group member. Group sessions can be dull, painful, and frustrating, just as they can also be exciting, joyful, and worthwhile.

All group members should commit themselves to attendance at all sessions and strive diligently to arrive on time. To join a sensitivity session, members must sign up in advance with the minister or "trainer."

Occasionally someone will assert that such training is dangerous. As outlined above, however there is absolutely no danger whatsoever.

We use the word "training," because this concept was developed as "laboratory training" several years ago. The setting is the "laboratory" and the members are the chemical agents. If the agents can be mixed in the right ways, the results can be most worthwhile. Each member then has an obligation to all other members.

Training for leaders of growth or enrichment groups is generally available for clergy through accredited programs. This can be a useful way to investigate the possibilities which sensitivity type groups can provide for a church. Background reading could include the following:

Robert C. Leslie, *Sharing Groups in the Church: An Invitation to Involvement* (Nashville: Abingdon Press, 1970).

Clyde Reid, *Groups Alive—Church Alive: The Effective Use of Small Groups in the Local Church* (New York: Harper & Row, 1969).

Ernest G. Bormann and Nancy C. Bormann, *Effective Committees and Groups in the Church* (Minneapolis: Augsburg, 1973).

Philip A. Anderson, *Church Meetings That Matter* (Philadelphia: United Church Press, 1965).

Saville Sax and Sandra Hollander, *Games People Ought to Play—Reality Games* (New York: Popular Library, 1972).

Howard Lewis and Harold Streitfeld, *Growth Games, How to Tune in Yourself, Your Family, Your Friends* (New York: Harcourt, Brace and Jovanovich, Inc., 1970).

Carl Goldberg, *Encounter: Group Sensitivity Training Experience* (New York: Science House, Inc., 1970).

COUPLES AND SINGLES CLUB

With the rising divorce rate we could not exclude singles from our "Couples Clubs." This in no way indicates that we should not have a club for singles only, as their need is great. The formation of such clubs is purely social.

You may begin a group with four couples or eight singles. Gather them together and plan eight monthly meetings with one person in charge of each meeting. The meetings should be held in homes. Choose eight homes. Discuss eight monthly Saturday night programs. The goal is fellowship.

The suggested programs following are having success:
1. Progressive supper:
    Choose four homes. The first home offers wine, cheese, and hors d'oeuvres or soup, depending on your religious convictions. The second home offers a soup or salad course. The third home offers the main course which is usually potluck, and the last home offers dessert. You may follow the supper by worship or program.

2. Bowling and pizza or Chinese restaurant night.
3. Swimming party and dessert in home of member.
4. Luau potluck in a home affording porch and view.
5. Clambake or picnic and beach party.
6. Old time movies or theater party and dinner out.
7. Dance, square dance, with meeting for dinner first.
8. New Year's Eve renewal of wedding vows followed by dinner and overnight at nearest luxury hotel.

You will note that the disciples ate together probably every evening up to the Last Supper. Eating together is a form of "communion" and most of the above programs are not costly.

Each meeting should involve four couples to be responsible for various aspects of the event. If they each invite one couple you will have a good group and good fellowship.

The club will grow from this basic plan. Once the group jells, it may wish to select officers and become involved in extracurricular events to help with church fund-raising and growth. Basically the group is for fellowship, getting to know each other, and attracting newcomers.

CHECK LIST FOR A HEALTHY CHURCH

A yearly inventory of what your church is doing or not doing in its total approach to parish administration can be both helpful and stimulating to the church leadership. If you notice a lot of blanks the chances are your church is not alive and growing.

BASIC FUNCTIONS
1. An established routine for Sunday worship   _____
2. Occasional special services of worship or evening services   _____
3. Church school, well equipped, for all ages, cradle to grave   _____
4. A good set of operating bylaws   _____

COMMITTEES
1. Governing Board elected according to parliamentary procedures yearly   _____
2. Worship Committee to aid minister or plan special worship   _____
3. Finance Committee to review expenses and plan annual pledge drive   _____
4. Religious Education Committee that meets monthly   _____
5. Membership Committee that meets monthly   _____
6. Social Action Committee that meets monthly   _____
7. Property Committee that meets monthly   _____
8. Publicity Committee that meets monthly   _____
9. Transportation Committee members available to drive those who need rides   _____
10. Hospitality Committee to greet people at the door of church and church school   _____

11. Coffee Hour Committee   _____
12. Committee of Ushers   _____
13. Church Decoration Committee—flowers, art, etc.   _____
14. Nominating Committee   _____
15. Denominational Affairs Committee, missions   _____
16. Music Committee to build choirs, hire professionals,
     purchase music   _____
17. Special Fund Raising Committee   _____
18. Committee on Adult Education, seminars, discussions,
     Bible classes   _____
19. Investment Committee   _____
20. Endowment or Memorial Gifts Committee   _____
21. Calling or Visiting Committee   _____

BASIC GROUPS
1. Women's group or groups   _____
2. Men's Club or clubs, dinner, luncheon, other   _____
3. Couples Club   _____
4. Singles Club   _____
5. High School Youth Group   _____
6. Junior High School Youth Group   _____
7. Golden Age Club   _____
8. Choir, Junior Choir   _____

BASIC STAFF
1. Minister   _____
2. Associate Minister   _____
3. Organist   _____
4. Janitor   _____
5. Secretary, or volunteer secretaries or clerk   _____
6. Financial clerk of pledge records records, treasurer   _____
7. Auditor   _____
8. Lay Readers   _____

PASTORAL CONSIDERATIONS
1. Stated office hours   _____
2. A telephone in the church office that rings in the
    pastor's home office, same number   _____
3. A well equipped study   _____
4. Counseling books, particularly marriage counseling   _____
5. Books in the field of Parish Administration   _____
6. Magazine subscriptions that aid in the minister's work   _____
7. Practice of lunching with church leaders   _____
8. Membership in service clubs or like groups   _____
9. Wall map showing your area and pinpointing new housing   _____
10. Pastoral calling a minimum of nine hours weekly   _____
11. Monthly open house at the parsonage for newcomers   _____
12. Telephone calls to members who miss church   _____
13. Attendance at local and denominational ministers meetings _____
14. Correspondence up-to-date   _____
15. Flexibility on occasion in worship services   _____
16. Structured time for sermon writing   _____

17. Personal social action _____
18. Educational stimulation by course or lecture _____
19. Job outline for secretarial work _____
20. Three hours a week on planning program, committee
agendas, group concepts _____

PASTORAL CONTRACT
1. Salary contract with cost of living clause _____
2. Pension plan _____
3. Housing plan _____
4. Car allowance _____
5. Health plan _____
6. Insurance plan _____
7. Vacation plan _____
8. Ministerial discretionary poor fund _____
9. Specific day off _____

ASSOCIATED GROUPS FOR DEPTH OF CHURCH INVOLVEMENT
1. Alcoholics Anonymous, Al Anon, Al Ateen _____
2. Boy Scouts, Girl Scouts _____
3. Yoga _____
4. Sensitivity Training _____
5. Parents Without Partners _____
6. NAACP or Urban League _____
7. Day Care for children _____
8. Great Book Club _____
9. Theater Group _____
10. Dance Group _____
11. Parent Education training in raising children _____
12. Discussion Club _____
13. Chess Club, Scrabble, Bridge Club _____
14. Church bookstore _____

FACILITIES
1. Sanctuary that is adequate _____
2. Church school classrooms, well equipped _____
3. Nursery, well equipped _____
4. Hall for functions _____
5. Kitchen adequately equipped _____
6. Parking lot _____
7. Minister's office _____
8. Secretarial office with adequate supplies, mimeograph, etc. _____
9. Well kept grounds _____
10. Attractive exterior buildings _____
11. Parsonage or manse or allowance for minister _____
12. Gymnasium, swimming pool, or athletic facilities _____

PUBLIC RELATIONS
1. Monthly or more often published newsletter to
all members and friends _____
2. Brochure specifically designed for your church for
newcomers _____

3. Pastoral calling cards, and prayer cards for hospital visits   _____
4. Attractive Sunday bulletin covers   _____
5. Adequate signboard with correct data in front of church   _____
6. Consistent newspaper publicity through paid events
   or on church affairs   _____
7. A good mimeograph machine   _____
8. A good mailing list and mechanical system for mailing   _____
9. Notices of your church services in hotels and motels   _____
10. Use of Saturday church page in local newspaper   _____
11. Use of radio or TV   _____
12. Up-to-date bulletin boards   _____

5
Adding New Blood to Your Membership

Bringing new members into your church will take a planned approach. Some churches have tried the "Sector Plan," others depend on ministerial door-to-door calling, and still others educate their members for intensive proselytizing. Here is a plan that is different, and has worked:

1. Set up a Membership Committee of five couples.
2. Plan and print an attractive brochure.
3. Schedule an Open House.
4. Plan your advertising.
5. Schedule a Church Family Dinner.
6. Plan a series of "Meet with the Minister Nights."
7. Involve newcomers into church activities.

THE MEMBERSHIP COMMITTEE

Set up a Membership Committee of five couples: three young married couples, one middle aged couple, and one older couple. The larger number of young couples is necessary because we generally are working with young married couples who enjoy making new friends their own age. Five couples is specified because during the year, five "Meet with the Minister Nights" should be scheduled in this program. The greatest asset of these members is the ability to greet new people cheerfully and warmly. No other qualification is necessary.

THE BROCHURE

Meet with your Membership Committee to spell out the plans for the year and to devise a brochure on church life. A three-fold brochure is best with dimensions that are 16¼ inches long by 8½ inches wide.

When folded twice into three separate sections it will fit nicely into a
9 x 6 inches manila envelope along with other pamphlets, or can be
mailed as is.

On the front of the brochure put a reproduction of your church. At
the top place the words: AN INTRODUCTION TO _____ CHURCH.
Under the illustration place the minister's name and degrees, the time
of Sunday worship and church school, the address, and telephone
number.

Upon opening the three-fold brochure the newcomer will notice one
picture of children in the church school, one picture of the Couples
Club, another picture of your Men's Club, or a picture of middle-aged
church members singing, ushering, or gathered for a meeting, or your
women's group in action. These pictures are surrounded by information concerning all the groups in your church. The basic principles
concerning all the groups in your church and the basic principles of
your church or Sunday school should not fail to be included.

When the three-fold piece is turned over, in the left column will be a
map showing the location of your church and underneath a picture of
your minister with a brief biography. In the middle column, a picture
of historical significance can be placed in the top left corner leaving
space opposite for the word "address" and a square for a postage stamp.
Underneath this space for the picture can be placed some church history or background. Because this section is the back page of the three-
fold piece, again include the time of your church services, and if there
is room, the name, address, and telephone number of the church again.

Have the brochure printed on offset, and print enough for a three-
year period. Try to plan your brochure to cover this three-year period
without making any changes. If you are not sure that your minister
will be with you for three years, do not include his name or picture. If
your committee is not budget conscious, you can plan a one-year brochure and include names of church officers, Sunday school leaders,
and courses, etc. But if you wish to save money, plan your brochure for
a three-year period. If you plan to give out and mail approximately 600
a year, you will find that an order of 2000 will not be prohibitive in cost,
and if you do the job right the first time, you may have the same brochure reprinted as is, far cheaper.

Brochures are to be handed out to newcomers at church or are mailed
out to new arrivals in the community, and can be placed in hotels,
motels, YMCAs, and other places of business, or on community bulletin boards, or distributed through Welcome Wagon.

THE OPEN HOUSE

The Open House should be set up for a fall date as a rule. The mobility of the people in your community will indicate the best date for your town. In the planned approach to church membership growth, the brochure coupled with advertising, should be dispersed about three weeks prior to the Open House. Your committee again should plan the date, time, and place of the Open House and send out engraved invitations to all prospective new members.

THE MEMBERS
of
FIRST CHURCH
cordially invite you to attend
an
OPEN HOUSE
on
Sunday, ____(date)____
in the Church Hall on Main Street
Your Town, State

The purpose of the Open House is to offer an opportunity to townspeople to come and to know your church better. Begin with a coffee hour and refreshments. Your Membership Committee is entirely present to greet and circulate. After the informal fellowship all are seated and hear the minister speak for fifteen minutes on the history, work, and theology of the church. Questions are raised and when the discussion subsides all return to the dessert table for further fellowship.

Although the number who attend such an Open House is often not great, you will be encouraged to find that nearly every one of those who attend will become a good member of your church in the days ahead.

PLAN YOUR ADVERTISING

Because your Membership Drive is detailed, so must the advertising be planned. A fall schedule might run as follows:

SEPTEMBER 1, Mail out your brochures. Place them in hotels, motels, and business establishments.

SEPTEMBER 4, Place a picture of your church in the paper. Under the picture print "Welcome to First Church, and to the morning service of worship at 11:00 A.M."

SEPTEMBER 9, Replace brochures as necessary.

SEPTEMBER 10, Place a picture of your minister in the paper. Under his picture the words: The Rev. Mr. John Doe cordially

invites you to attend morning worship at First Church and then
to join him for dinner at noon. No admission charge will be
made. All welcome.

SEPTEMBER 11, Have a spot announcement on the radio welcom-
ing the public to your church family dinner. (If this is your
"Rally Day" give that adequate coverage also, and your attendance should be record.)

SEPTEMBER 14, Mail out invitations to your Open House.

SEPTEMBER 16, Place the open invitations in local places of notice.

SEPTEMBER 17, Place the picture of your church and the minister
in the newspaper and extend an invitation to the public to attend your Open House.

SEPTEMBER 18, Have a spot announcement on the radio inviting
the public to your Open House. Extend an invitation from the
pulpit as usual.

SEPTEMBER 19, Open House.

SEPTEMBER 22, Mail your handwritten invitations to newcomers
who have attended church and invite them to the home of a
member for a "Meet with the Minister Night" on September 29th.

The dates are important and timing is a key factor to success. Consistent advertising at constant intervals is most effective. In advertising, a picture is still worth a thousand words. Not everyone will read
your copy, but every reader of the local newspaper will see the picture
you present.

THE FAMILY DINNER

The "Family Dinner" can be planned for any date in line with your
every member canvass. Thanksgiving Sunday is an excellent date for
a "Church Family Dinner" where the public is invited free of charge.
The dinner must be well planned by your Dinner Committee. The food
should be donated by the members. If every member is called to bring
something you will be assured of a fine attendance and a joyous occasion. I need not go into the details of a pot-luck dinner. If your budget is
no problem, then the dinner should be catered, so that all church members may have fellowship with each other and new arrivals. Your
membership committee, as always, must circulate and greet all.

THE MEET WITH THE MINISTER NIGHT

Young couples today enjoy being together. A call by the pastor in the
afternoon on the wife alone is normally not nearly as effective as a call
on both in the evening. But the minister cannot go out every night lest
he break down physically, or neglect his own family. The problem is at

least equally difficult for women ministers. This problem is greatly alleviated by nights set aside by the Membership Committee to meet in their homes to bring together four or more young couples at once for a talk with the minister. All that is necessary is a home. Choose the most spacious available. The Membership Committee handwrites the letters of invitation and makes telephone calls the night before the gathering to see how many are expected. The committee members serve dessert and clean up after. The minister talks directly about the church and its program and answers questions. New couples meet others and make fast friends. No evening spent on church work is as profitable as these to the growth of the church. Every newcomer is invited to attend these "nights." Usually more than half your newcomers respond gladly to the evening out with others of like interests and intentions and come alive with you.

INVOLVEMENT

Throughout the entire program of your membership drive there is ample opportunity to involve newcomers. They are readily and painlessly involved in the Family Dinner, the Open House and the Meet with the Minister Night. This involvement has a great effect on the new arrivals without them even being consciously aware of it. Your hospitality and your welcome have touched them and they are thankful to be a part of such a beloved community. They are involved at this point and it takes little nudging to involve them further. You will be pleased with the response when you ask a newcomer, who has followed your fall program, to sing in the choir, usher, teach Sunday school, or join the church.

Involvement is the climax of your program. Without it you will have failed. Involvement is the final step of the new member to commitment and dedication to your church and your God. Your church membership form should list all the ways a newcomer can become involved.

Next time your Membership Committee meets, make plans for your drive. You will be greatly pleased with your results.

6

Building a New Church, or Old Wine in a New Bottle

Before a congregation actually builds a new structure there are some important factors to consider.

The congregation desiring to build must have a real need, and that need should be translated into obvious factual statements. The need, with the correct statistics to back it up, should be spelled out clearly. The need should be talked about and presented lucidly until the entire congregation is aware of it. Let us look at a few illustrations:

a) *We need a new religious education building.* Why? Because we have 165 children in our Sunday school with an average attendance of 110. We have ten grades. These children all meet in *one room,* our vestry. Some have met on the stage and in the boiler room and in the choir loft. We have no nursery where young people can leave their children while they attend church (consequently they do not attend often). Our teachers find it difficult to teach because of the noise, the temporary quarters, the lack of blackboards, and general facilities. We are not attracting young people because it is not readily apparent that we are prepared to educate their children. A well-organized Sunday school with adequate facilities will attract young families. We need a new religious education building.

b) *We need a new hall.* Our last Church Fair was not as successful as it might have been because we had so little space. It is not adequate for our youth groups, couples and singles clubs, our Men's Club, or for our women's groups. It is not large enough for a church family supper. It is not serviceable for Scouts, other service groups, or for large assemblies. We need a hall to meet these needs.

c) *We need a new church sanctuary or auditorium for worship.* Last year we had to have two services and still we averaged close to seating capacity. On Christmas and Easter and on Family Sundays there was not enough room. Mr. and Mrs. Brown reported that they stood in the hallway during the services on those religious holidays. Our choir sits in the balcony, our organ is old and decaying, the pews are falling apart, and the altar is not large enough for a wedding ceremony. We need a new place in which to worship.

d) *We need a new church location.* We are located in the city, there is no parking space. Our attendance is very poor and we are not attracting new families. Statistics reveal that the average young couple will not travel over two miles to go to church, and the potential all live in new homes about three miles away. Our building is in poor condition. We are located in a business zone, and our Church Board reveals that the land is worth $90,000.00. Thus we can sell the present building and build a new church out where the new families are locating.

These examples are common. Compiling and studying the exact statistics is necessary. If the *need* is honestly and lucidly presented to the people, they will arise to meet it. The next question asked follows logically:

How Will We Raise the Money?

Money is raised on the basis of NEED. If people recognize the need of the church to receive and their need to give, the money will be raised.

Once you have decided to build a new church, do NOT draw plans and project cost figures.

An over-zealous committee may draw plans and pictures and set costs. When this is done and presented to the congregation it is not always met with enthusiasm. Often a good giver will take one look at such a plan and highly disapprove of it. You have lost his gift *before* you have even asked for it. This happens too often. The money should be raised on the basis of *need,* and *need only. After* it is raised is the only time to project a plan.

In considering the raising of funds, optimism should prevail. According to some fund raisers' estimates, the average church can raise ten times the amount presently being given to the operating expenses over a three-year pledge period. Thus a congregation raising $9,000.00 a year for operating expenses can raise approximately $90,000.00 over a three-year period! This money is raised at the same time the $9,000.00 is being raised as usual. Some churches even increase their budget giving during the three-year period! It is a well established fact that a professional fund raising organization of good reputation offers the church the best opportunity to meet its needs financially. It is strongly suggested that you consider the services of a professional church fund raiser. He will know how best to handle your particular situation with your help. His services are invaluable. He will help you to train a good corps in canvassing procedures which can be used for years to come. Such training aids your future canvasses immeasurably.

If you decide to "go it alone" do so on the basis of your past experience in fund raising. Do your people give freely? Have your "Every Member Canvasses" been highly successful? Do you have at least twenty well trained canvassers? If you can answer yes then you might try to go ahead alone. It is not the purpose of this chapter to set forth fund-raising procedures, but a few additional points are important. In conducting your own canvass you should have two trained men for each five families. For example, if you have a membership of 300, divided into 150 pledging units you will need not less than twenty-six canvassers. They will be composed of one chairman, five teams with a captain for each team. These people should be trained to make personal calls and to have the *needs* well outlined in their minds. They should all canvass one another in advance and should be top givers. Before the canvass begins the amount already pledged by them should be announced. Remember, no canvass is ever really completed until there is a detailed report on every single person listed.

In raising money for buildings or improvements, it should be kept in mind that a failure on the first attempt often proves disastrous. Your congregation becomes unnerved and discouraged. The money already pledged will not come in as it should, and you will have trouble convincing anyone that you ought to try again. If this occurs, drop the project until the *need* really hits your congregation square on, in the future.

It is the above point which often tips the scale toward choosing a professional fund raiser. He will do the job right the first time, as a rule. Some companies will even guarantee to raise approximately seven times your present giving to operating expenses.

After you have raised the money on the basis of the NEEDS, another factor looms most important.

Select a Good Building Committee

In selecting a good committee for building, the usual rule—"keep a committee small for efficiency"—should not apply. All of your people will be interested. Often interest follows after someone has given money because he wants to know how you are going to spend his gift. Choose a committee where all groups are represented, especially the Sunday school leaders, and add to this group of representatives your specialists. If you have an architect, a contractor, a painter, a plumber, etc., let them express themselves. Some churches form sub-committees.

One group sees the Sunday school needs, another the worship needs, another the hall needs, etc. The sub-committees make detailed reports on their needs and how they feel they can be best filled. A large committee is cumbersome, but it will pay off in a job well done to the satisfaction of the largest number of people.

The committee should plan to meet the greatest needs first. Do not make the mistake of trying to build an *all purpose building*. By this is meant a building wherein rooms serve double and triple purposes. The room that serves many purposes usually doesn't serve any one purpose adequately. If you build a hall and divide it into classrooms with folding doors, you are making a mistake. Those who have taught Sunday school know that there is no substitute for an individual classroom: displays are not moved, blackboards are stationary, supplies are always handy, noise is at a minimum, and teaching is enjoyable in such an environment. It is even easier to get teachers! If you build a chapel for the worship of your Sunday school, put stationary pews in it. It is not good to have to set up chairs in a chapel that was used the night before for a youth group dance. It is difficult for adults to worship in a supper hall with a cross thrown onto a table hurriedly covered by a red cloth. We should not expect our children to worship in such a room. Build your building so that it meets your specific needs.

There are some areas that do serve double duty. A large classroom may serve as a youth room or projection room where two classes could view a filmstrip. A large hall may serve for scouting, recreation, church suppers, assemblies, and dramatics. It should not be divided by folding doors unless it is absolutely necessary. A children's chapel is often considered a luxury, but its use is great. All youth groups can conduct their own services in it. A children's choir sings on Sunday morning. It is used for small weddings, funeral services, special services, and private baptisms. The main thought is that we should not build a new building to serve all purposes, for then it serves none. It is better to meet one need at the right time than to try to serve all partially. A good building committee will plan to meet the greatest needs first and fill the lesser needs the best they can. If the *needs* are well outlined, this will not be difficult.

In conclusion:

• Have the needs clearly defined and well understood by your congregation.

• Choose a good fund-raising organization and raise the money on the basis of *need* alone.

• Choose a good committee to do the job right the first time.

The Regional Church

One design that is currently attracting considerable attention particularly as transportation improves, is the regional church. Some people hold that it will only be a matter of time until most denominations recognize the value of a regional church. In an age of regional schools, suburban shopping centers, parking problems, and superhighways, the centrally located church will emerge as a strong possibility.

It is a well known fact that people will drive to a shopping center miles away if they are assured of getting what they want. In rural communities the regional school has been the answer to the question of how to provide the best in facilities and teachers at the lowest cost to each member community.

The parking problems of some of our city churches are so great that they might consider relocation on this basis, and coupled with an outmoded building in disrepair, relocation seems inevitable.

The American landscape is dotted with outmoded rural churches. Most of these rural churches are struggling for survival. Nearly all of their members travel some distance to the church. It is in the rural areas that the regional church is most needed, and the urban area churches will in some instances be forced to follow their lead if they wish to serve a mobile population in these fast-changing times.

A city that has more than one church for every fifteen hundred of population is an over-churched city, and growth potential will be negligible. Some churches must remain to serve the inner city but a cursory survey will reveal that most of our American cities are over-churched and many with buildings bearing the *same denominational name!*

When three or more churches of the same denomination are within two miles of each other in a congested city, and two or more of these buildings are in disrepair, as well as being located in the "business property" zone, we see an ideal situation for merger and planning for the regional church.

An analysis of the largest growing suburb of such an over-churched city will reveal the best location for the regional church.

The new church should be located within a two-mile radius of the largest amount of construction of new homes, as close to the city as possible, and yet within five miles of a third community population. This type of location is not difficult to find.

In rural areas many prime locations for the regional church are available. Quite often such a church can be located on the border of three different townships and within easy driving distance from the center of each of these townships. Occasionally such a church can be planted directly in the middle of four or more townships with access roads.

What would the regional church offer? Some of the features are very appealing:

— an easily accessible church for the largest number of people.
— a sanctuary for the worship of five hundred.
— a children's chapel to seat two hundred, and twelve classrooms of various sizes, including a modern nursery.
— a gymnasium that would double for an auditorium (with a stage), and a banquet hall, with kitchen.
— at least one phase of organized recreation for all ages, such as bowling alley or indoor swimming pool.
— a minister's office designed for counseling, a church office for supplies and printing, and a secretary's office with files.
— a church library for adults and children.
— a lounge with fireplace and kitchenette for board meetings, fellowship, and small group meetings.
— a youth room complete with record player, television, encyclopedias, and a study corner.
— adequate rest rooms and closet space and a zoned heating system.
— a parking lot designed for the easiest entrance and exit of 300 cars, with room for expansion as necessary.
— its own bus for member transportation as necessary.
— a well-designed landscape of trees, shrubs, and gardens with a place for outdoor meditation and worship services, and if possible be situated at the top of a gently sloping hill.

The reader may add to this list as his dreams take shape. Such a regional church is really within the realm of possibility *today* for many of our denominations.

Once the church was the center of the life of the community. The regional church can again make the church come alive as the center of all persons' lives.

Picture, if you can, a hillside on the outskirts of the city. On this hillside we shall build a church. It will be a complete "church" in every sense of the word. The church building will house every conceivable church-related activity. It will be surrounded by landscape and beauty. The vast parking area will be unobtrusive. The spire will be visible for miles around.

It will only be a matter of time until our denominations recognize the need for a "regional" church. A church that would serve a dispersed population covering both suburb and city over several miles. In an age when regional schools and suburban shopping centers dot the landscape to the advantage of multitudes, a regional church will also rise to serve these same persons. In an age of parking problems and superhighways it is deemed a pleasure to drive out of the congestion to reach a desired end.

Occasionally a city church will move to the suburbs. Too often, however, the church building is built upon a small lot, the parking lot is not large enough, there is no room for expansion, and the building itself is grossly inadequate. If a church is going to build, it should build right the first time, or not build at all!

In the words of Christ:

> "For which of you, desiring to build a tower, does not first sit down and count the cost, whether he has enough to complete it?" (Luke 14:28)

Many of our newer church buildings indicate a lack of vision, a reticent faith, and a stingy congregation not willing to truly build for posterity.

When locating the regional church the land area, which should cover at least two acres, should be within easy driving distance of the newest and largest housing development, and on the best access road from the nearest city. A detailed study of the land area is vital. In many areas of America, a regional church can easily be located within one mile of the city limits, and between two fast growing suburbs, as well as being within one mile of a new housing development.

In our rural areas, we need only give as much thought to the location of the regional church, as the townspeople gave to the location of the regional school. We might find that we can quickly develop an unsurpassed *youth* program if the regional church were across the street from the school! In our rural churches many farmers and residents already drive a good distance to their struggling little churches. Many rural churches close their doors every year. If all of these churches had pooled their resources and built a regional church, the spiritual impact would be wonderful on the entire population.

The regional church located outside the center of a community is perhaps the best way to again make the church the center of the community. It would become the center of the community because it would offer every outlet for human expression and aspiration. The regional church would stand out as a symbol of all that is good and as an outstanding symbol of religion in America.

One model of the regional church might include the following features in its floor plan. This design would not fit every congregation's

KEY TO THE REGIONAL CHURCH

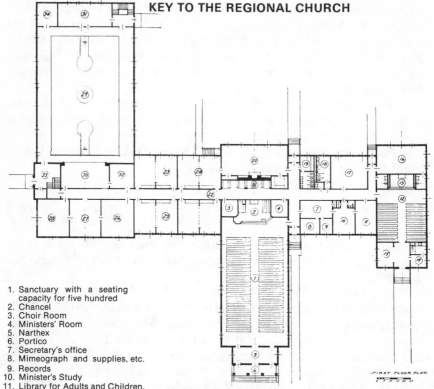

.FIRST FLOOR PLAN.

1. Sanctuary with a seating capacity for five hundred
2. Chancel
3. Choir Room
4. Ministers' Room
5. Narthex
6. Portico
7. Secretary's office
8. Mimeograph and supplies, etc.
9. Records
10. Minister's Study
11. Library for Adults and Children, Displays, Exhibits
12. Chapel, for use of children, youth groups, small weddings, and funerals, seating 160
13. Chancel of Chapel
14. Brides' room, powder room etc.
15. Reception room
16. Kindergarten
17. Nursery
18. Mens' toilet
19. Ladies' toilet and powder room
20. Lounge to be used by adult groups, women's groups, small lectures, receptions, etc. (kitchen in right foreground), fireplace
21. Coat and hat area with folding doors
22. Corridor
23. Primary Dept.
24. Primary Dept.
25. Junior Dept.
26. Youth Room including television, record player, study desks, encyclopedias, religious periodicals, etc.
27. Senior Dept.
28. Adult Dept.
29. Assembly hall, gymnasium

30. Stage, chairs and tables stored under stage
31. Kitchen
32. Stage dressing room

33. Vestibule, stairway to pool and bowling alleys, locker room and Scout room
34. Storage room

SUB-LEVEL
The swimming pool would be directly under the gymnasium.
The meter room under the vestibule.
Mens lockers under room 32.
Womens lockers under room 23.
The bowling alley under rooms 26, 27, 28.
The Scout room under room 25.
The boiler room under room 20 is centrally located.
The remainder would be unexcavated.

PLAY YARD
Play yards may be placed directly by the nursery or primary rooms. They should be cut off from the parking lot by dense shrubbery or rose fence.

OUTSIDE WORSHIP AREA
An area for worship out-of-doors should be one of the primary assets of the regional church. Place in relation to lot size and beauty.

RECREATION AREA
A large lot can also afford an outside area for recreation, scouting, Sunday school picnics, ball games, etc.

DRIVEWAY
This should circle the church with entrance and exit signs discreetly placed. A driveway coming up to the portico would be advantageous.

These plans can be expanded as one's dreams take shape. The present plans are in the realm of possibility *today* for many of our denominations.

needs, but it indicates the comprehensive scope that is needed in church planning. Other approaches are available from Stanmar, Box LC1, Sudbury, Massachusetts 01776. This organization has prefabricated buildings to suit almost any budget or need. It will also redesign basic plans to fit a church's specific needs. Another source is the well known church consultant and design firm C.A.S.E., Inc., P. O. Box 24, Glenn Dale, Maryland 20769.

7

New Approaches to Financial Life

In working out a financial structure for the church program, the minister and officers should give special attention to the need for an effective every member canvass.

This chapter includes first a list of nine basic qualities which characterize a successful every member canvass. It may be helpful to check out your current program by reviewing these qualities. If your church shows a need for improvement in any of these areas, you might think seriously about the value of trying a different approach.

1. The needs of the church should be presented clearly. Fund raising efforts are always dependent upon needs. They should be easily spelled out for all who are expected to contribute. In this way the approach can be made in a positive, objective manner that is never negative or overly emotional. It is better to list three needs that all are aware of than it is to list twenty that parishioners do not fully understand.

2. The canvass plan should be well detailed. Every member should know the plan and be aware of exactly what will take place and when it is expected. A simple plan which is well followed is better than an elaborate plan that falters. Plan October through November dates.

3. The canvass plan should be followed to the letter. Too much change may indicate that the plan was not prepared thoroughly. It also tends to confuse members of the congregation and dampen their enthusiasm.

4. Members who give sacrificially should be invited to serve as canvassers. The feeling that money begets money applies here. Those who know the value of generous giving and practice it add a

vital element of excitement and their example encourages others to strive to meet their standard of giving. Keep in mind also that it is more important for the member to know the canvasser than it is for the canvasser to know the member. Therefore, canvassers should be well known church leaders.

5. The every member canvass should usually include a congregational dinner. This occasion often called a "fellowship" or "loyalty" dinner tends to unify the congregation in its effort.

6. The canvass committee should consider the value of answering early pledges that are substantial in size. Without mentioning names, the announcement of early, pace-setting pledges and even the total pledged by the canvass committee could have a healthy effect and spur the canvass on in an optimistic fashion.

7. The canvass should be limited to a very definite period of time. It is advisable, for instance, that the canvassing itself not last longer than two weeks.

8. The "follow-up" should be well timed and executed. No canvass is complete until the job is finished. This means that even though reports from some giving units may be a disappointing "no pledge" or "pledge when able," the canvassers should make definite reports within the time frame.

9. The results should be announced promptly.

If your review of these nine qualities of a successful canvass lead you to think of new ideas, you might go over the list with your church officers. In turn, you may decide together that it is time to put new life in your church finances.

The four models of canvass plans which have been used successfully can supply additional information to your officers and to the canvass committee. The point is that it is important to develop your own plan, one that adequately meets your situation, and helps your church to reach its objectives.

These four include: face to face solicitation, canvass by telephone, canvass by mail, and the home canvass. Following these models, the chapter includes sample letters which can be used or adapted to fit your situation. Each of these letters illustrates a different way for arriving at a congregation's financial goal and they should be studied carefully. This is an important, preliminary step and each congregation must determine its financial objective in a reasonable manner.

FACE TO FACE SOLICITATION

OCT. 1   Send for Pledge Cards and Offering Envelopes as needed.

OCT. 2   The Finance Committee meets to plan the canvass. They appoint the entire committee (generally some of the most loyal givers). They set forth a date outline of events. They ratify the budget and compose a letter to all members to introduce the canvass. They appoint a committee to plan for the Fellowship Dinner.

OCT. 3   Letter is mailed out to all parishioners announcing the coming canvass and including a date outline of events.

SAMPLE LETTER

Dear Friends of First Church:

We all have one thing in common, a real concern for our Church. Each year we conduct a financial canvass to meet the needs of First Church. Our Sunday school needs your support. Our building fund grows daily with your help. Our pastor needs your financial encouragement. Our plan for this year is . . . .
(Date and details)

We thank you for your past yearly support. We know you will do your best to keep our church active in the year ahead.

Faithfully yours,
Finance Chairman

Names of Canvass Committee

OCT. 9   Full Canvass Committee meets to set the total canvass goal. This is done through careful study and analysis of previous church receipts and expected church needs. After the goal is set a letter is composed to send to members and friends of the church. The letter states the canvass goal and the needs of the church and urges recipients to give generously. There are numerous ways to decide upon the goal for your "Every Member and Friend Canvass." The sample letters at the end of the chapter illustrate this process. A similar letter should be sent as a second mailing from the church office.

OCT. 10   The second letter is mailed out to all announcing the Fellowship Dinner and enclosing budget and goal of canvass.

OCT. 14   The Dinner Committee divides mailing list, telephones all units, invites them to sit at their table, and offers transportation to the dinner on May 22.

OCT. 16   Full Canvass Committee meets and divides new pledge cards and offering envelopes among themselves. They do not have any stated amount on the pledge cards. They receive some instruction on how to make the face-to-face canvass. The Dinner Committee meets also to complete plans. The dinner should be catered and free if possible. The third letter is composed stating the needs of the church clearly and urging all to attend the dinner.

OCT. 17   Third letter is mailed out to all, stating the major "needs" of the church. Do not list many needs, only the three most important.

OCT. 22   The Fellowship Dinner takes place from 7–8 P.M. and is followed by a principal speaker who briefly outlines the needs and who in turn is followed by the canvassers who are some of the most well known members of the church. They tell briefly why they have pledged generously. Dinner ends at 9 P.M. Baby sitting is provided free.

OCT. 27   PLEDGE SUNDAY. Canvassers meet for luncheon following the Sunday service of worship. (Luncheon by Dinner Committee.) Canvassers hear brief pep talk and go out for face-to-face solicitation. Canvassers return to church at 5 P.M. to report.

NOV. 2   Key leaders attend to the follow-up as necessary after hearing final canvassers' reports. (No canvass is completed until every single unit is reported on.)

NOV. 11   Canvass results are announced.

CANVASS BY TELEPHONE*

(For Small Churches)

OCT. 1   Send for offering envelopes with pledge cards inserted.

OCT. 2   Finance Committee meets and chooses units to be included in the telephone canvass. Letter is composed explaining canvass approach. Budget is included on separate sheets. NEEDS are clearly set forth. Three needs are emphasized. Do not list too many needs.

OCT. 3   Letters, envelopes are mailed out.

OCT. 6   PLEDGE SUNDAY. Following morning worship the canvassers will call parishioners and receive verbal pledges and record same on duplicate card. (A church secretary may even be used.) Results announced on the following Sunday and in the church news letter.

*In such a canvass, everyone must know that they will be called on the phone on Pledge Sunday and be ready to state their pledge. All the "facts" have been included in the May 3 mailing.

This can be a one-day canvass and it is all over, or follow-up can be planned by governing board.

CANVASS BY MAIL

OCT. 1   Send for Pledge Cards and Offering Envelopes. See that the cards are IN boxes of Offering Envelopes.

OCT. 2   Meeting of Finance Committee, Church Board, and any appointed canvassers. Choose the units to be canvassed. Compose a letter listing the *needs* of your church, and tell exact canvass plans. Include the budget.

OCT. 9   Mail out Offering Envelopes with pledge card in them and a letter giving full information.

OCT. 20   PLEDGE SUNDAY. All members attend church and place their pledge cards in the morning offering plate. Have additional pledge cards in the pews.

12 P.M.   Full Canvass Committee meets following worship and the canvassers divide up the names of those *not* pledging and go out to make face-to-face calls.

3 P.M.   Canvassers report back to church.

OCT. 27   Canvassers meet again following morning worship and make the final follow-up and report back at 5 P.M.

OCT. 28   Results are announced.

THE HOME CANVASS

OCT. 1   Send for pledge cards and envelopes.

OCT. 9   Finance Committee meets.

1. They select those to be canvassed.
2. They choose one home for each twenty units, and call to confirm availability of that home for the Canvass Night.
3. One member of the Canvass Committee is chosen to speak in each home.
4. Each host and hostess in each home is given the list of guests for personal invitation by letter and by phone.
5. They compose a letter explaining the canvass. It will include the names of the hosts and hostesses and who is to be invited to each home. It will include the budget and a listing of major *needs*.

OCT. 11   The letter is mailed out with all pertinent facts—budget needs, type of canvass, etc.

OCT. 14   The hosts and hostesses call and mail handwritten invitations.

OCT. 21   CANVASS NIGHT or Pledge Sunday parishioners arrive in the homes and are served dessert and coffee (8–9). The speaker talks about the Church Needs, and then hands out the boxes of offering envelopes with the Pledge Cards included in them. Those present are asked to sign the cards and to place them in envelopes. These are collected and taken by someone from each home to the church or to a central location. The church treasurer opens the envelopes, totals the pledges, and telephones the result to each home. The average pledge per unit is announced.

Refreshments are again served to all, and fellowship takes place, or everyone may be invited back to the sanctuary for worship and celebration.

OCT. 25   Full canvass committee meets and makes follow-up as necessary by phone or door-to-door solicitation.

This approach has a unique advantage of integrating the membership. The fellowship can be enjoyable and unifying. The mutual support of other members encourages a more cheerful pledge procedure. This canvass instills the team effort. Meeting in homes of members is neutral ground and therefore pressure is not nearly as great. The togetherness of those present stimulates mutual help and concern for the work of the church. The home atmosphere often can do what the church atmosphere inhibits.

The home offers a unique opportunity to relate in whatever way seems natural and appropriate for those present, and it lends a freedom of speech and discussion that cannot be found anywhere else.

Defining the Canvass Goal

These letters illustrate alternatives that can be followed in presenting the canvass goal.

Dear Members and Friends of First Church:

We have decided not to set a canvass goal this year because the sky is the limit.

Our church budget will be realistically detailed after YOU have decided upon your pledge.

If you wish:

TO SUPPORT OUR MINISTRY
TO BUILD A STRONG CHURCH SCHOOL
TO EXPAND OUR CHURCH PROGRAMS

then pledge as much as you possibly can on Canvass Sunday.
Our budget and our future depend upon YOU.

With faith and hope,
Your Finance Committee

(Signed) Chairman's name

Dear Members and Friends of First Church:

We have set our canvass goal at $25,000.

This realistic figure was reached by adding a four percent increase to the amount we raised last year. Four percent was chosen due to inflation.

Last year you contributed $24,000 to our church. The average yearly pledge was $240 and the average monthly pledge was $20.00, for a weekly average of $5.00.

We still have one hundred pledge units and to reach our goal every unit should consider a 4% increase just to keep us even with inflation.

For those who desire to support our minister and our church programs and to expand our work please consider raising your pledge on Pledge Sunday.

We have great hope for this coming year.

Thank you,

(Signed) Chairman's name

Dear Members and Friends of First Church:

We have enclosed a realistic budget for the coming church year. The budget needs have given us our canvass goal.

Our goal is $30,000.00

We have a potential of one hundred pledge units and this indicates that we should consider an average pledge of $300.00 yearly.

When considering the average pledge we must realize that many cannot meet the average, while many others will exceed the average. We recognize a danger in specifying an average yearly pledge because some may feel that they have been giving beyond the average and may consider lowering their pledge to the standard. We are also aware of an annual 14% loss due to circumstances or parishioners moving away.

Yet, there are many who ask, "How much should I pledge?" and others who do inquire as to the average pledge so we offer this data for your serious consideration.

Our ministry needs your support.

Our church school needs your gift.

Our programs need your contribution.

Please do the best you can for your church.

Yours in Christ,

(Signed) Chairman

Dear Parishioners:

We have enclosed a budget for your consideration. When we subtract investment income and other approximate incomes we find that we still need $30,000 in pledges.

Our canvass goal is $30,000.00.

Your finance committee feels certain that we can meet this goal if every pledge unit contributes _____ percent of their annual income.

The national average gift to the church last year was approximately _____ percent of income and we feel that our giving has always been above average.

Our ministry is above average.
Our church school is far above average.
Our church programs are growing above average.

Please consider pledging your fair share to your church.

Sincerely,

(Signed) Chairman

(Signed) All Committee members

Dear Members and Friends of First Church:

We have established a canvass goal of $30,000.

In 19__ the average weekly income in our nation was approximately _____ yearly. It is our feeling that our church membership is slightly above the average.

If every pledging unit gave __ percent of the average national yearly income to the church, religion everywhere would thrive. This average gift amounts to $_____.

We have one hundred pledging units and if each unit contributes $_____ we would exceed our goal, and our church would thrive in the year ahead.

Please consider giving three percent of your income in return for that which God has given to you.

Thank you for your thoughtfulness.

Sincerely,

(Signed) Canvass Chairman

Note: Each church may fill in the blanks accordingly.

Each letter has a different emphasis so that readers can combine or alter their letter to their situations.

Note the following data:

1. All letters fit on *one* page with margins.
2. No letter lists more than *three needs*.
3. Inflation may be mentioned.
4. The average expected yearly pledge may be suggested and the danger.
5. The average yearly loss of pledge income or raise by late pledgers may be stated.
6. A percentage of income can be used, varying from the average gift to a tithe.
7. The budget may be enclosed with the letter.
8. Notice the salutation includes "friends."
9. Every letter should be *signed* by hand by the chairman. If this is not possible the stencil may be signed for reproduction.
10. Write an optimistic ending. Your "Every Member and Friend Canvass" or "Parishioner Canvass" must be uniquely designed by your committee for your particular church. Give it a good deal of consideration.

8

Bringing Pastoral
Life to the People

The basic principle in pastoral calling is to accept a person where he is and to lead that person to higher ground. The following concepts apply to "Parish Visitors" also.

Calling often looms as a monumental and never-ending task. Who to call on next and why can often be a complicated decision. Random calling without rhyme or reason is ineffective calling. Calling should be an organized affair, not a hit-or-miss proposition.

The following questions should be asked:

What is the purpose of calling?

How many calls should be made?

Who should be called on and how should we respond to each call?

WHAT IS THE PURPOSE OF CALLING?

To let people know you care about them and to accept them where they are

To remind them that the "church" cares about them

To bring a religious point of view

To build a relationship of trust and loyalty

To offer your help as necessary

To overcome misunderstanding arising in the church relationship

To give hope and courage to the sick

To give faith and insight to the dying

The most important element in all pastoral calling is to convey a sincere concern for another person. Calling is effective only when based on a position of mutual respect and trust. The parishioner must feel that the caller truly cares. Religion as such will not be as effectively communicated during a call unless the pastor and parishioner are in the process of building a real friendship. This friendship is basic religion.

Once the person-to-person relationship is established, the pastor may attempt to meet the needs of the parishioner.

HOW MANY CALLS SHOULD BE MADE?

Most pastors start out with great expectations. They set goals for themselves that are truly impossible. It is far better to set a minimum goal that is realistic. In order to set a calling quota a minister should operate on some sort of weekly schedule as suggested in chapter one. Calling will be an integral part of a weekly schedule that will include stated office hours, committee assignments, worship services, and all other duties.

As a rule, morning office hours are a necessity for good parish administration and for making the pastor consistently and readily available. Night meetings are more and more common, not only for the pastor but for many parishioners. Night calling, to be truly appreciated by all, should be scheduled in advance and during weeks when night meetings are fewest.

The best calling hours are generally from 12:30 to 4:30 on weekdays. If the pastor takes one day off, this will leave four afternoons with a total of sixteen calling hours. In relation to setting the calling quota at a realistic minimum, three calls an afternoon should be scheduled. A good parish call will generally take up an hour and often much longer. By this schedule the pastor may make nine to twelve calls a week. In some churches a three-day calling week with a goal of nine calls for a forty-eight week total of four hundred thirty-two calls a year is considered quite adequate. A church that requires more than five hundred calls a year is a church that needs an associate or assistant pastor.

WHO SHOULD BE CALLED ON AND
HOW SHOULD WE RESPOND TO EACH CALL?

At the beginning of each week the pastor should review the entire mailing list carefully. At this time he may recall those who are becoming less active or who may be sick, troubled, or in need of concern.

It is suggested that calls be made in the following order of preference:

1. Sick
2. Troubled
3. Shut-in
4. Newcomer
5. "Strategic" parish call
6. Routine parish call

The Call on the Sick

There is a saying that "the sick are always in." Often when the scheduled calls do not materialize, a sick call may be repeated, but not overdone. Sick calls are generally short calls.

The basic principle of calling applies: accept the patient as he is, and lead him to higher ground. Thus, the minister, as the doctor, usually asks how the patient feels. If the patient is unable to talk, an appropriate prayer may be delivered. If the patient cannot hear, he or she may be given a three by five card with an appropriate prayer on it. The prayer also should keep in mind the basic principle. It should begin by the acceptance of the suffering and move into areas of health and hope. An example of such a prayer is as follows:

> O Thou art the source of strength,
> In our weakness and misery we come to Thee—
> Our hearts are heavy with discouragement, and we have too little faith.
> Help us to know that we are not alone,
> That Thy love is here with us and around us—
> We would ask Thee now:
>> For patience in suffering,
>> For the faith that conquers pain,
>> For the courage to face our sickness boldly.
> Help us to recall fond memories.
> Help us to dream new dreams.
> Help us to see ourselves well again that we might live life anew with Thee.
>> Bring us strength to recover.
> Lead us onward in hope.   Amen.

Such prayer usually ends the visit.

If the patient is able and willing to communicate, the pastoral call begins with a concern for his or her feelings. Let him talk about his misery without interruption, and never with any comparison of his illness to another's. Remember it is improper to pry or to ask about the illness. When the patient has vented himself, lead him gently into areas which help him to think of recovery and activity. In a well-performed sick call the pastor will readily note the transition from the acceptance of misery to the areas of new thought on "higher ground." Often this transition is obvious when at the beginning of a call a patient will say, "I don't think I'll ever get well," and then when the pastor leaves he says, "I wonder when the doctor will let me go home?" or the patient might say, "Gee, I'm looking forward to fishing again." When this occurs a good sick call has taken place. Pastors should not feel guilty if no "formal religion" seems to have been conveyed. Such "religion" should have been instilled when the patient was well, and if it was not, your presence and sincere concern *is* religion, and your ministry a symbol of your church's concern and of your God's concern.

The Call on the Troubled

This is a call on those who are troubled about their relationship to the minister and the church.

"Troubled" parishioners are common. They feel they are misunderstood, they are gossips, backsliders, paranoids, frustrated, the "trouble makers" and their church relationships are usually anxious ones.

All pastors know that they should call on their dissenters and critics as soon as they are aware of same, yet too often this call is put off. This call is placed second in importance to "sick calls" because it is often disastrous if they are not made.

At the first sign of dissent a pastor should call. The basic rule applies: listen patiently and intently to the dissent, then carry the call into new areas of constructive thought. This call takes listening above all else. The unhappy, anxious, and frustrated church member is usually just as anxious in other areas of his or her life also. He will not go to you in these areas, but he does expect you to go to him in relation to his church. It is not so much *what* he is unhappy about but that he feels no one *cares*. Your care is very important and is usually all that is necessary for peace. Such persons need more care than others and are often habitual dissenters. An empathic pastor knows when to make such a call *before* trouble starts. For "the troubled" can cause a lot of heartache and misery for pastors if they are not alert and concerned. Pastors generally feel that troubled parishioners dislike them. This is usually not the case! Quite the contrary is generally true, troubled parishioners feel that their pastors dislike them. This point must always be kept in mind.

The Call on the Shut-In

Shut-ins are usually elder members who have given a great deal of time and substance to our churches in the past. These persons should not be neglected. How often they are visited depends on how filled the calling schedule is. Shut-ins are easily pleased by a call and such calls can be very helpful and instructive to pastors entering a new church.

A call on the shut-in follows the basic rule above, but will be more interesting and friendly if the pastor is up on all the latest news about who is doing what and why. Shut-ins relish all kinds of gossip and thus the minister must be discreet in giving the news. Such sessions often call for a good sense of humor, funny incidents about children are generally pleasing. These calls can be handled well by appointed parish visitors.

If the shut-in is ill follow the basic rule of accepting his or her illness and suffering and then going on into areas of hope and meditation. The prayer should be concerned with eternal and everlasting stability more than with the acceptance of suffering as in the "sick call" because the shut-in has generally accepted his illness and is awaiting death. The prayer should be grounded in the infinite.

> O God in whom we live and move and have our being, we know that Thy presence is with us.
> Help us to know that out of Thee we emerged, with Thee we live, and at death we still live with Thee.
> Thy spirit runs through us and within us and Thy love supports us now and forever.
>
> Amen.

The Call on the Newcomer

In their zeal to bring in newcomers many pastors spend hours calling on strangers and new arrivals. Often such calls are not fruitful and are made at the neglect of other church members. Church growth is often more productive if young couples are trained to make calls on other young couples. In many instances it is advantageous to have a young couple open their home and personally invite newcomers to a dessert night at which time the minister can talk to them about the church. This method enables the minister to see four to five couples in one evening and has the further advantage of having young people meet other young people.

Calls on newcomers generally have to be made at night to see both husband and wife and should be scheduled in advance. Use a two way postal card. The call on the newcomer should not be long or pushy but a warm, direct, and brief welcome to attend the church.

The Strategic Parish Call

The strategic call is designed to further the goals of the program of the church and parish administration.

Such calls are the rule in the big business world where face-to-face confrontation produces real results.

In the operation of the church the minister should meet frequently with key members. A pastor will thus make a call, appointment, or luncheon date with such key persons in order to inform them of plans, ideas, and to solicit support for specific projects. During such a call the layman should be asked for his backing. The lay member should be encouraged to attend important meetings and give support to the minister assuming he or she agrees with the action. Financial canvasses, building operations, and other important church action is greatly enhanced by strategic calls on key persons who are generally pleased to be included and confided in. Such calls build strong relationships and mutual respect and confidence between pastor and key church members.

Strategic calls are often useful to sense the feeling of the majority in relation to changes in church policies. A minister may meet with a key layman who will speak about the change of policy with other good members to assess their feelings and whether or not the time is ripe to instigate new action. The slow leaking of information for public reaction is common in political circles. Who leaks the viewpoint and how is important. Assessing the feedback is vital.

Strategic calls are political in a sense but quite practical in many instances. As with any strategy it can fail miserably. Such calls should be purely motivated and carried out with all facts available. Such calls are not devious but open, candid, honest, and practical approaches to very complicated and important problems. Strategic calls make for a live church.

The Routine Parish Call

Generally the pastor tries to enter the home of every member at least once a year.

Many active church members are called on last because the pastor sees them often in church-related functions. Sometimes they do not need your visit at all. If this is true, a *note* can occasionally be written commending them for their activity, or a *telephone call* can produce the desired effect.

The routine call is a call to establish strong bonds of friendship.

It should be well publicized that the pastor will call on any person upon request and respond to such a request immediately.

The following notations may be helpful when making calls:

1. Introduce yourself and the name of your church *clearly*.
2. Notice the type of home you are entering: landscaping, pictures on walls, books in view, hobbies noticeable. Establish areas of mutual concern.
3. Ask who the people are and about their family. Who are they related to in the church or community? What are their interests?
4. Discuss their past locations and church affiliations.
5. Discuss their reason for coming to your church. Or discuss their present duties in the church.
6. Discuss the church program and offer some printed material.
7. Express a desire to see them in church some Sunday.

In summary, remember the basic rule: accept the person as he is and lead him to higher ground. Your main objective is to show a real concern for those called upon. Follow the rule and convey your concern and the church will come alive.

Pastoral Geriatrics

As we find that people are living well beyond seventy, the ministry to the elderly is increasing daily.

Experienced pastors know that one of their first duties is to call on the aged members. Many of these people have given much time to their church in younger years and still contribute and attend with a loyalty not seen in many younger members.

Indeed, many of the elderly are just that, in the sense that they are always constant in their church relationship and add balance and dignity to a congregation's deliberations and growth. The busy pastor often overlooks the depth of the contribution made by the elder members just by their presence in church, Sunday after Sunday. Many younger persons enjoy the view of senior citizens. Young men often seek out the advice of the elderly in their businesses.

No church would be whole without its older members, and ministers should be thankful for their steadfast loyalty, year in and year out, in bad times as well as in good. Naturally, however, the elder members present some problems: senility, infirmity, and immobility. The shut-in elder is a constant concern—his or her demands on a pastor's time increase.

Many ministers know that if they call once a month on eighty-two-year-old Mrs. Brown, who is senile from hardening of the arteries, that she will want them to call one a week. Sometimes a shut-in will demand a call once a day. There are even times when Mrs. Brown will telephone only one hour after the pastor has left and say, "When are you coming to visit me?" She will already have completely forgotten the visit.

There are also times when the minister will neglect a call on the senile because: "She doesn't know me any more; she doesn't even know where she is." Occasionally this is true. Mrs. Brown *acts* as though she doesn't know anyone, except deceased loved ones, but she still may be more knowledgeable than we suspect. Even though her conversation rambles and she repeats the same question over and over, the presence of the minister has its calming effect. Mrs. Brown, who was curt to Doctor Jones, may sit up and eat for her minister. The person who was rude to the caretaker may show real poise and manners for the minister. In most cases, the pastor's call can be a steadying influence on a senile person.

All of the elderly shut-ins, senile or not, enjoy talking about old friends and others who are shut-in that they know. This healthy gossip is a tonic to the soul and unites them with others in a unique way. The pastor or parish visitor would do well to catch up on this healthy gossip before calling on any shut-in.

"A picture is worth a thousand words" is especially true with the shut-in. They enjoy having pictures of their minister and the minister's family; they enjoy pictures in the weekly bulletin, and many an older person has pinned the Easter, Thanksgiving Day, or Christmas colored bulletin in a place of prominence. An alert pastor will always be ready to ask a question about the picture of someone on the wall of the shut-in's home. A good paraphrase of the well-known quote is: "One picture leads to a thousand words."

Calling on the shut-in takes time. Very little satisfaction will come from any call that lasts less than an hour. This rule applies whenever the shut-in is able to sit up and converse freely. Any shut-in can sense when the call is routine duty or prompted by real Christian concern. A brief call on an elder member, who craves fellowship, is a thoughtless injury to the shut-in. Once a minister decides to stay one hour or more, all anxiety is alleviated and the call will be gratifying to everyone. No "clock watching" on this call, as on any other. Schedule your time as any good professional person should and do the job right. It is an eye-opener to note that our best and busiest doctors are generally the ones who still give their patients undivided attention and time. It is also noted that it is the busy pastor who has to follow some doctors into the sick room and engage in a good conversation with the patient because the doctor did not find time.

Many churches are able to structure a calling committee of elderly able people who can visit the shut-ins as a supplement to the pastor's visits. These active elders can bring all the news and besides they have similar interests and anxieties.

One of the anxieties of the elderly is death. Some keep asserting, "I didn't ask to live this long; why can't I die?" Others are afraid to die and will seldom mention the word. Still others blatantly threaten suicide. The nursemaids and caretakers of the infirm elderly often toss off remarks flippantly. "Oh, don't talk that way!" or "I won't let you die, sweetie." The minister should be alert in this area and face the problem of death with the patient, and thereby help the elderly *accept* the fact of death calmly and reasonably. It is not what the pastor says, but whether or not he or she can act secure in the thought of death and convey his or her faith and trust in God. It is the open honesty with which we face a problem that others avoid that is helpful. To elude the discussion of death when the elderly brings it up, or to change the topic of discussion is only to increase the anxiety of the dying. When death is brought up, discuss it.

In calling on a shut-in:

Plan to give at least an hour of your time.

Accept them and their feelings as they are.

Talk of old times as they wish.

Use pictures to advantage.

Tell them what their contemporaries in the community are doing.

Don't avoid the topic of death and use prayer as necessary.

Go over your church mailing list often to make sure that you have not forgotten "one of the least of them."

9
Saving Life
Through Counseling

There are at least three interesting stories relating to the three basic types of psychotherapy.

Relative to Freudian counseling, a patient entered the office and lay on the couch. He refused to speak. The psychotherapist with his back to the patient is trained not to speak either, so nothing was said. The patient left and paid his fifty dollars for his "fifty-five minute hour."

The next week the same patient returned. Again he lay on the couch and said nothing. The doctor said nothing. The patient left, paying his fifty dollars to the nurse.

The third week the patient arrived; he lay on the couch. He said nothing. The doctor said nothing. Fumbling for his fifty dollars in his pocket, he finally spoke: "Do you need a partner?"

Traditional psychoanalysis involves practically no words on the part of the therapist. The process takes three to five hours a week for three to five years. Very few ministers practice psychoanalysis.

Most ministers were weaned on the works of Rogers' non-directive psychotherapy. In this type of counseling the minister is taught to listen a great deal and to elicit positive response by saying, "I see," "That is interesting, tell me a little more." Or the words of the patient will be repeated.

There is a story about a parishioner who entered a pastor's office. The minister had been schooled in Rogerian, non-directive psychotherapy, and after a warm greeting, silently awaited the first words.

The parishioner said, "I feel lousy."

The minister said, "Oh, you feel lousy."

The parishioner said, "I've got an awful headache."

The minister said, "Oh, you have an awful headache?"

The parishioner said, "I feel like pacing the floor," and began to do so.

The minister made no response, but watched stoically.

The parishioner then climbed on the window ledge and said, "I feel like jumping out the window."

The minister said, "Oh, you feel like jumping ten floors out that window?"

Whereupon the parishioner jumped and died.

There is a point at which we must be directive in our counseling, especially if someone is about to harm themselves or others. Only experience can tell us when to be psychoanalytical and say nothing, when to be non-directive, or when to be directive.

William Glasser in his book, *Reality Therapy* has openly defied all tradition by calling past trauma garbage. His emphasis is more directed to "Who are you?" "What are your capabilities?" "What is your duty or job?" and "Let's get on with it, with no excuses."

This is a direct approach. The counselor alone has to decide when to use it and when not to. Counselors have to be unafraid to take risks. If you are afraid to take risks and if you do not feel qualified to enter into psychotherapy, then you should have names and phone numbers to which to refer people.

After several years of counseling, ministers will find that they will be both passive and active, as experience dictates. Active or not, they will learn that they should be shocked by nothing, make no judgments, and show very little anxiety. They will have devised their own counseling method, and they will continue to practice and grow.

Basic fundamentals include a well located, soundproof office, and an approach to greeting counselees which is cheerful, open, and honest. The necessary textbooks relative to marriage counseling, alcoholism, child counseling, and psychotherapeutic counseling should be in the office and carefully read and studied. Among the books may be these:

William Christian Bier (ed.), *Marriage: A Psychological and Moral Approach* (New York: Fordham University Press, 1965).

Silvano Arieti (ed.), *American Handbook of Psychiatry* (New York: Basic Books, 1959).

Felix Deutsch and William F. Murphy, *The Clinical Interview* (New York: International Universities Press, 1955).

Rollo May, *The Art of Counseling* (Nashville: Cokesbury Press, 1939).

Karl Menninger, *Man Against Himself* (New York: Harcourt, Brace and Company, 1938).

Lewis Robert Wolberg, *The Technique of Psychotherapy* (New York: Greene & Stratton, 1954).

Ethel (Sabin) Smith, *The Dynamics of Aging* (New York: W. W. Norton, 1956).

Richard M. Steiner, *A Guide to a Good Marriage* (Boston: Beacon Press, 1955).

Seward Hiltner, *Pastoral Counseling* (Nashville: Abingdon, 1949).

Wayne E. Oates, *Pastoral Counseling* (Philadelphia: Westminster Press, 1974).

Seward Hiltner, *The Counselor in Counseling* (Nashville: Abingdon, 1950).

Howard J. Clinebell, Jr., *Basic Types of Pastoral Counseling* (Nashville: Abingdon, 1966).

Wayne E. Oates, *New Dimensions in Pastoral Counseling* (Philadelphia: Fortress Press, 1970).

Ian F. McIntosh, *Pastoral Care and Pastoral Theology* (Philadelphia: Westminster, 1972).

Wayne E. Oates and Kirk H. Neely, *Where to Go for Help* (Philadelphia: Westminster, 1957, 1972).

Charles F. Kemp, *Pastoral Counseling Guidebook* (Nashville: Abingdon, 1971).

Howard J. Clinebell, Jr., ed., *Creative Pastoral Care and Counseling Series* (Philadelphia: Fortress Press).

Russell L. Dicks, *Successful Pastoral Counseling Series* (Englewood Cliffs: Prentice-Hall).

William E. Hulme, ed., *Pocket Counsel Series* (Philadelphia: Fortress Press, 1971).

The minister should have ready at all times the names of doctors and psychiatrists to whom he or she can refer those who are too emotionally disturbed for general pastoral counseling.

Three areas of concern come most frequently within the counseling experience of ministers: marriage problems, alcoholism, and child adjustment problems.

Marriage Counseling

The marriage counseling interview usually begins when a very distraught wife calls the minister on the telephone. As counseling should not generally take place by telephone, the minister should make an appointment as soon as possible for one hour and meet the wife at his or her office at the stated time. The wife should be told to make this appointment known to her husband.

The husband, in many cases, responds with anxiety and reluctance. It must be made objectively clear to him that his wife feels their marriage to be in trouble and that such a step is necessary. He may later go to the minister or not, as he wishes. It is generally felt that working with one partner in a marriage can be helpful. If that one person can understand why she acts as she does, or why her husband seems to follow a certain pattern in their marriage, a better marriage can be built. There can be no transformation in a marriage relationship until the partner is accepted as he or she is. Acceptance can yield transformation.

On the first interview the minister will listen and take notes. If the counselee rejects note-taking, the minister should upon the wife's departure make notations as accurately as possible.

This first session will be one of catharsis. The minister will listen and at the close of the first interview try to structure the course of the counseling. The counselee will be asked if she has found the meeting fruitful. Would she like to continue for a period of three months? She will further be asked to explain her need for counseling to her husband and tell him that the minister is ready to see him whenever he desires.

On the second interview the counselee will again vent herself, and at the close of the interview she will be given a form for her and her husband to fill in. (*A Marriage Adjustment Form*, by E. W. Burgess, reprinted by Family Life Publications, Inc., 219 Henderson Street, Post Office Box 427, Saluda, North Carolina 28773. The materials from Family Life are available to counselors and ministers. Laity can request that a minister order them.)

The form will be returned on the third interview. It is hoped that her husband will also have done this task thoughtfully. Whether he does or not is a sign as to his readiness to come to discuss his married life.

Between the third and fourth interview, the minister will study the form carefully along with any notes taken and see what insight can be gained and what interpretation might be made for discussion with the counselee.

Generally, by the fourth or fifth session, the husband will become so curious or interested in the process that he will give some indication of wanting to see the minister. He will be greeted cordially and will usually speak reluctantly. If he seems at a loss for words, or angry, the counselor should explain that counseling can help people to paint an objective picture of their problems. Seeing the picture more clearly often helps them to build a better marriage. It should be explained that the counseling experience should be a determined effort over a period of at least three months and that his wife feels that it will be helpful and it is hoped that he, too, will agree. If he agrees, his appointments may be scheduled for every other week or more frequently if urgency dictates.

It is generally felt to be a good idea to let the counselee know what to expect from the counseling situation. He will meet with the minister for an hour because a longer time has been found to be only repetitive and not fruitful. He will not be judged. His words will be kept in strict confidence. The type of counseling is non-directive and supportive and includes insights and interpretations as they are. The following pages or a similar outline defining the procedures that will be followed will be given to both partners.

ABOUT MARRIAGE COUNSELING

1. The spouse who initiates the relationship will attend three sessions of one hour each. That spouse will inform the mate that he or she has entered into counseling and the mate shall decide whether he or she wishes to enter also.
2. After the initial session it will be agreed that the counseling commitment will extend to a period of at least three months. The time may be extended beyond this if required.
3. If both partners commit themselves to the three month period, they will be seen on alternate weeks for one hour sessions.
4. Printed forms will be used, particularly, *A Marriage Adjustment Form*, for the purpose of objectifying specific areas of discord. Bibliotherapy will be used when it seems appropriate.
5. One *rule* will be followed throughout, namely that *all* three persons involved in the counseling will be as honest as possible with each other, having the right to openly discuss what each person says to the other. The counselor will use discretion in repeating anything said, but the goal is open, honest dialogue. Each partner is encouraged to relate as accurately as possible what was said in his or her counseling session to the other as soon as possible on the same day. This approach teaches objective communication between partners.
6. Any transference of love or hate to the counselor will be discussed and worked through. Counter transference will be discussed at the session following its use.
7. Most sessions will be non-directive, i.e. the counselor will LISTEN and elicit articulation. However, directive counseling will take place as necessary, especially after the initial sessions. The directive counseling may involve homework which implies that one partner may be asked to do some specific act which all agree might be helpful and renew growth in the relationship.
8. Three goals should be kept in mind: COMMUNICATION between partners, ACCEPTANCE of one's partner as he or she is to bring about transformation, and the uncovering of PATTERNS of behavior, many of which may be carried over from childhood.
9. Occasional psychological interpretations *will* be made by the counselor. Dreams, early traumatic experiences, sibling rivalries, relationship to parents may be discussed. Behavior patterns may be classified as psychic masochistic, compulsive, obsessive, sadistic, etc. The counselor will readily admit fallibility and interpretations will be discussed thoroughly when made. Such interpretations prove valuable to those having a background in basic psychology, are not "dangerous" when worked through, and do help self-awareness and changes in behavior patterns. The counselees will be encouraged to practice introspection.
10. There will be no judgment made on the part of the counselor in respect to sin. Basic ethics and morals will be discussed as relevant.
11. Clients who act out or display psychiatric syndromes or psychotic tendencies will be referred to a psychiatrist. The counselor will still play a supportive role if the client and the psychiatrist agree.

12. At the end of the three month period there will be a summarization of the patterns, problems, and stresses in the marriage and how they might be coped with. A report, in writing, will be read and discussed and presented to the couple for study. If they decide further counseling is necessary another three month session will be planned.
13. This paper will be given to all who enter counseling for study, and a discussion of the procedures is encouraged.

For Those Considering Divorce

More than one-third of all marriages in the United States end in divorce. Many remarry and find themselves still unhappy and unfulfilled.

Divorce is a serious step in a lifetime. It should not be entered into lightly or inadvisedly. A checklist like the following might help to open communication in counseling.

CHECKLIST

1. Underline the reasons why you want a divorce.

Adultery	Alcoholism	Homosexuality
Physical violence	Drug Addiction	Sadism
Disease	Mental illness	Masochism
Desertion	Hate	Impotence
Bigamy	Lust	Sex
Money	Greed	In-laws
Religion	Loss of respect	Incest
Others		

2. Underline the reasons for marrying.

Love	Intelligence	Sex compatibility
Companionship	Trustworthiness	Manners
Desire for children	Integrity	Status
Good provider	Stability	Cheerfulness
Personality	Shared activities	Religion
Others		

3. Underline the reasons why you stayed married as long as you did.

Children	House	Sex
Financial security	Material possessions	Good provider
Retirement plans	Grandchildren	Good homemaker
Community	Religion	Relatives
Others		

4. Do you know the divorce laws of your state?
5. Do you know how much a divorce will cost?
6. Are you prepared for a single life and the loneliness involved?
7. If you are a woman, are you prepared for a career other than homemaking if you have to work?

8. If you divorce will you have to sell your house, car, boat or other material possessions?
9. Where will you live?
10. What advantages will single life offer you that you do not now enjoy?
11. What kind of settlement and/or alimony do you expect?
12. Do you mind living alone?
13. Will a divorce break up many friendships?
14. Do you have hobbies?
15. Are you running away from something or to something?
16. Is menopause a factor in your decision?
17. If you have children, how will the divorce affect them?
18. How will you handle the visiting rights of your mate?
20. Will you be living in the same community after the divorce?
21. Do you feel that your first spouse will keep entering into your life after the divorce?
22. If you remarry, how will your new mate react to your children?
23. If your new spouse has children of his or her own, how will the children relate to all parents involved and to each other?
24. Do you feel that all parties in a divorce and remarriage can honestly be good friends?
25. If you plan to remarry, what can another mate offer you that the first spouse did not?
26. If you plan to remarry, can you objectively list your own personal faults and failings in your first marriage?
27. If you have a prospective mate in mind, do you know his or her faults and weaknesses?
28. If your prospective new mate has been married before, do you know why that marriage broke up?
29. If you enjoyed extra-marital sex how enjoyable was it?
30. If sex is a factor in your divorce, did you ever discuss it with a knowledgeable counselor?
31. Do you honestly feel that neither you nor your prospective new mate will not bring past behavior patterns, faults, and weaknesses into a new marriage?
32. If you plan to remarry, what time period will you consider in order to get to know a new mate?
33. What do you hope a new spouse will offer you?
34. If you have been cheating on your mate with your prospective mate, what makes you think that he or she will not continue those cheating ways after your second marriage?
35. Does a new mate really offer you anything that your present mate has no potential to develop?
36. Where do you picture yourself ten years from now?
37. What could you do twenty years from now with a new mate that you could not do twenty years from now with your present mate?
38. Have you seriously planned for your retirement years?
39. How will your relationship to others who are close to you be affected by divorce?
40. Have you both been through a minimum of three months of marriage counseling?

CAUSES OF DIVORCE

The author's personal experience after twenty-six years indicates that the major causes of divorce in their order of importance are as follows:

1. Lack of communication leading to repressed hostility and misplaced anger.
2. Money worries.
3. Differences of opinion as to raising the children.
4a. Sex without imagination.
 b. A loss of the natural child.
5. Possessiveness and jealousy.
6. Marital ruts because of lack of thoughtful imagination and structured vacations and shared activities.
7. The retention of bad memories with an inability to forgive and forget.
8. Nagging.
9. Loss of individuality and necessary freedom.
10. Taking each other for granted.

All of these factors should be discussed in the marriage counseling setting.

Alcoholism

Alcoholism is one of our country's most serious problems. Doctors generally find great frustration in their experience with alcoholics. Psychiatrists find that alcoholics take a great deal of time that could be better spent with other patients.

Alcoholism has been termed an illness. Alcoholics Anonymous seems to have the greatest amount of success with the problem. (For pamphlets published by Alcoholics Anonymous, write to Alcoholics Anonymous World Services, Box 459, Grand Central Station, New York, New York 10017.) Every minister should have a goodly supply of pamphlets from AA in his church pamphlet rack for parishioners to take freely.

It is generally agreed that alcoholics are often childlike in their approach to daily living. They sometimes enjoy being mothered. They tend to lie easily under stress. Their oral fixation is symbolic of unconscious problems, and alcoholism is a form of suicide. (See Karl Menninger, *Man Against Himself*, pp. 160–184.)

The alcoholic will come to the minister usually under the influence of alcohol, or immediately after a binge when suffering from remorse, and occasionally with thoughts of suicide. As is true in most cases of counseling, you can help only those who truly desire to be helped. This desire on the part of the alcoholic is likely to be fleeting.

When the alcoholic does come, treat the person with kindness and sympathy. Gently but firmly guide the counselee into the nearest group of Alcoholics Anonymous. If he or she refuses to go, it is hoped that the minister can sustain contact and see the counselee again on a specific date for pastoral counseling. Some alcoholics may wish to continue the counseling relationship while they are getting started in Alcoholics Anonymous.

The wife or husband of the alcoholic must be given information on the subject and should discuss the problem of alcoholism thoroughly with her or his minister. The mate must be willing to attend AA meetings with the wife or husband.

If the alcoholic refuses help from AA and wishes counseling, the minister should take the proper courses of study and develop a good library.

The alcoholic can continue to be a pastoral problem for many reasons: (1) the alcoholic may not be able to afford psychiatric treatment, (2) there are too few alcoholic clinics, and (3) the family will continue to come to the minister for help. Alcoholics should remain closely related to their church and their religion. They need constant support in a verbal sense and should be kept as active in as many things as possible.

Listed below are some generalizations of opinions from noted authorities:

Sigmund Freud: Alcoholism stems from strong oral childhood needs not met, "oral fixation." Drinking causes a regression to childhood states whereby the drinker can derive pleasure in thinking and acting without logic.

A. A. Brill: Both Brill and Freud also implied that there may be a repression of homosexual traits in some alcoholics.

Edward Glover: Alcoholism carries with it sadistic drives and oedipal conflicts.

Benjamin Sachs: Alcoholism serves to bring a compromise between hysterical and obsessive-compulsive neuroses.

Sandor Rado: Alcoholism emerges out of depression and alcoholics often seek elation from drinking.

Karl Menninger: Alcoholism is an attempt at slow suicide, self-destruction.

S. G. Klebanoff: Alcoholism emerges out of feelings of inadequacy, fears of failure that are internalized, and deficiencies in social relationships.

Harry M. Tiebout: Alcoholics have an unconscious need to dominate coupled with feelings of loneliness and isolation.

Robert P. Knight: Alcoholics suffer from a character disorder dis-
played by excessive demandingness, repressed hostility and rage,
and the inability to carry on with sustained effort. Alcohol pacifies
these frustrated needs.

Personality Characteristics

Some of the basic characteristics of the alcoholic personality follow:
1. Alcoholics have a *low frustration tolerance*. They desire immediate
   gratification.
2. Alcoholics are generally *sociable* people. Their relationships are
   superficial.
3. Alcoholics have feelings of *inferiority combined with attitudes of
   superiority*. They feel they should have preferential treatment,
   speak of their importance, and yet basically feel they are "no good"
   regardless of their accomplishments.
4. Most alcoholics are *fearful* persons. They are afraid of anything
   which poses a challenge. They expect to be treated with derision
   and disrespect. The ability to accept the respect of others is a sign of
   potential recovery.
5. Alcoholics are *dependent* people. Some will regress to childlike dependency, others will reject being dependent and brag of their mas-
   culinity or strengths while others lie between the two extremes of
   denial of dependency and complete dependency. The latter group is
   most treatable because they are still flexible, they are not afraid to
   admit their dependent feelings, they have a healthy fear of being
   too dependent, they recognize their state of conflict and attempt to
   deal with it.

It is recommended that you read *Frontiers of Alcoholism* (New
York: Science House, 1970) edited by Morris E. Chafetz, Howard T.
Blane and Marjorie J. Hill. Therapy involves as much "doing" as
psycho-dynamics. Alcoholics Anonymous meets dependency needs
and involves action. Psychotherapy must be firm and gentle at the
same time and extremely patient and constant.

Child Counseling

The minister will soon discover that a task tangled with frustrations
will be that of dealing with children of parishioners. Few counseling
experiences can bring about more criticism. Parents are often jealous
of the minister who can attract young people and cannot generally be
counted upon to help the minister in counseling problems with young
persons unless their understanding is fully given before the counseling is structured.

The child will generally tend to exaggerate what the minister suggests. For example, a seventeen-year-old girl who was told by her minister that he felt there was nothing wrong with a girl her age staying out on a date until eleven o'clock told her parents, "The minister says I can stay out as long as I wish with any date on any night." The minister was faced with an angry parent. When trying to explain what really had been said, the parent retorted, "Are you calling my daughter a liar?"

Another child was asked to write an essay about the man whom he most admired. The boy chose to write about his minister. When the father read the paper he was filled with jealousy and anger, and his relationship with his minister, thereafter, was never the same.

Many ministers have failed in the discussion of sex with youth group members. The minister must be very careful about receiving the blessing of the parents before entering this field.

Children of any age feel more secure and adjust to life more happily if they know there are adults who care about them, other than their parents. Wise ministers make themselves known to the children in the church. They should conduct worship services for them regularly. They should sit in on Sunday school classes as time allows. They should meet with the youth groups when feasible. Their counseling with children will not be with the psychotic child, or the retarded child, it will be with normal children who are going through the stages of growing up, but at certain stages seem to cause teachers and parents much anxiety. The relationship of the minister to such a normal child will be that of a close friend.

Some exaggerated phases are common—the eleven-year-old boy who thinks everything is stupid; the twelve-year-old girl who breaks into tears for no apparent reason; the teenager who doesn't want to do anything; the seven-year-old who is preoccupied with thoughts of life and death; the eight-year-old girl who wants to know the facts of life; the thirteen-year-old from a wealthy home who is caught shoplifting; the twelve-year-old boy who is caught drinking liquor; the fourteen-year-old girl who feels she is in love with an older man. There are many phases that the minister should be aware of and help both child and parent understand.

The parents will often consult the minister first if their children are doing poorly in school. This seems to be the most serious maladjustment of the child from a parental viewpoint. "Why doesn't George behave in school?" There may be many reasons. He should have a complete physical examination including thyroid. If he is fine physically, we can ask to talk with George if he wishes. We can watch him in Sunday school class or in youth group. We can arrange to see him privately before Sunday school on Sunday morning if we have the time. Since George was coming to church anyway, this approach lends itself more easily to give and take, and it is not likened to some other special appointment which might give him anxiety.

A mother brought her child to my office early one Sunday morning and I greeted him with boy talk about football, fighting, movies, and TV until he was sufficiently relaxed to begin talking. In less than fifteen minutes he was telling me of the death of his father and how worried he was that his mother might become sick again and place him in an orphanage. I told the mother of this anxiety and suggested that she reassure him that she was not likely to get seriously ill and she would not place him in an orphanage. Charles' conduct improved greatly after this brief interview and on that same Sunday he wrote a message on the bulletin board that related to my sermonette to the Sunday school, "Charlie loves everybody."

Child counseling then is related to how easily the pastor can make good friends with children. Once the friendship is well established the child talks readily about anything.

In counseling teenage girls, as in counseling adult women, the male minister should be extremely careful that the "transference" of affection, if such occurs, should be explained. The counselee should be fully aware that such transference can take place and that if it occurs it will be used constructively. Many ministers will prefer to avoid transference by asserting that their relationship is platonic, strictly, counselor-counselee.

The male minister should always be aware lest he be openly seduced by a frustrated girl or woman. Occasionally a mere pat on the back in a reassuring way will be imagined as an advance. Teenage girls will occasionally feel that you care for them by the slightest word or gesture, and when this is reported to their parents a great deal of trouble can ensue.

COUNSELING THE CHILD IN THE HOSPITAL

Four year old Alan was failing fast. He had been lying in a hospital crib for nearly a week gasping for breath in his struggle with pneumonia. He hates his new environment; to get back at those who have placed him there, he refuses to eat. He had gained much attention from this approach in the past and feels now that this mood will again bring results. The nurses come often, forced smiles upon their faces, asking him to eat. He refuses with zippered lips. Their authority is overbearing. Alan could not feel that they truly cared about him as much as they pretended. He refused to eat for his parents who had placed him in his jail. They would come to him during visiting hours, with a bowl in one hand and a spoon in the other, pushing the spoon to lips that he would never open. He was too weak to stand, but that didn't bother him. It was the confusion in his mind, the empty feeling of being left behind by those he loved. He wondered if he would ever get home again and hope was nearly gone.

After a long, long time a man who Alan vaguely remembered entered the room. He had seen this man somewhere before. The minister smiled warmly; he was not fidgety or nervous. Alan knew he was a friend, he felt it. When this man asked Alan to eat, Alan ate.

The explanation for Alan's eating so suddenly is not easy to come by psychologically. Alan might have felt that his parents had deserted him. He might have felt that they had put him away as they had threatened to do when he was bad. He may have felt he was being punished for some misdeed. In Alan's case, he felt that he would never go home again. The minister recalled a past association which had been happy, his church. Alan felt that this man could restore that past to him. He knew the minister was not responsible for his confinement and was thereby a true friend. He trusted this friend and eating for him came naturally.

Some parents are able to remain rational and calm as they place their children in the hospital; they are fortunate. They find it easy to make explanations even to very small children. Their children feel that they are not being abandoned. Even though some children may not understand why they are there they "feel" that their parents have the situation under control and will save them from danger and return them home.

Three-year-old Nancy waited to hear the steps of her mother coming down the long corridor. She had only one question in mind: "When can I go home?" She had asked the question before and received the same answer, "Pretty soon." "Pretty soon," to Nancy, meant an hour from now. She had already been in that awful place one night and that amounted to a long time; another night would be a long, long time. When Nancy's mother finally arrived she again heard the same words, "Pretty soon." The words were becoming to mean "Never." Nancy was heartsick. They were all lying to her. Even her doctor and some of the nurses were parroting, "Pretty soon." Her faith in grownups was faltering and there was no one to save her and return her home. So Nancy lay there restless and wondering.

There are parents who are fully aware that a child's sense of time is not the same as an adult's. According to psychiatric research our sense of time is not fully developed until fourteen years of age. For many adults one week in the hospital is a long time—how much longer it would seem for Nancy. Children do have a way of facing facts. They expect their parents to tell them the truth and to thus share the experience with them. The answer to Nancy's question might well have been a "long, long time" from Nancy's point of view. The cliche "pretty soon" had become meaningless and the deception kept Nancy constantly wondering if she would ever go home. The frank answer, "I don't know," with the reassuring statement, "But, you *will* go home," is one that maintains mutual trust between parent and child.

I remember seven-year-old David who found out that he was going to be in the hospital to have his tonsils removed. He became very pensive. When his mother asked him what was worrying him, David replied, "I don't mind going to that hospital but don't let them palm off a baby on me like they did to you the last time you were there." David, like many other children, has many preconceptions about just what goes on in a hospital.

Dennis was eighteen months old. He was lying in a strange bed with white sheets and white witches were tending his broken leg. His room held three other cribs and each contained a crying child, so Dennis cried too. His parents had been coming to see him but only for a few minutes, and they always left without him. Each time they left he wailed at being deserted again, and all his companions wailed with him. So Dennis lay there, he did not understand why, suffering miserably.

Because Dennis had not yet learned to communicate, his parents didn't bother to try to explain to him just why he was there. They came and visited, rubbed his back, held his hand, and then left. Some parents are aware that even children who cannot talk or do not have a good vocabulary do understand something from explanations. Somehow a verbal explanation makes them feel that their parent has the situation under control. Some children between the ages of one and two can actually understand the necessity to be hospitalized, even though they will not like it. Words spoken clearly and calmly do bring confidence to small children who apparently don't seem to comprehend the exact meaning of the words. An attempt to explain, without anxiety, is a worthwhile endeavor.

There are some hospitals that do not allow parental visits. Their experience has indicated that the child can accept hospitalization better if he is not visited for an hour and then left in tears and frustration, often causing a relapse of symptoms. Nurses are often overheard saying that a parent's visit has done "more harm than good." Other hospitals disagree. They allow parents to sleep in and to care for the child. In some sections of the Children's Hospital in Boston parents are offered kitchens to prepare food and to feed their children and can stay with them daily. Many parents know that their child cries violently when they leave the hospital bedside, yet they feel the visit is important. If they can somehow communicate to the child in word and manner that they have the situation under control and that the child *will* return home they can help the recovery. Quite often clergy of all denominations will become adept at such explanations and manner. *These ministers will plan to arrive at the time visiting hours are over.* They will calm the child and report to the parent. They are free in most hospitals to visit at any hour.

As a result of measles complications and dehydration fifteen-months-old Brenda was in the hospital. Being a typical one-year-old her reactions were negative. She had only recently learned how to drink from a cup and refused the bottle. The nurses, not knowing this, had left her bottle in her crib. Brenda did not touch it. Becoming sicker, without the much needed fluids, she was fed intravenously. Her arms were filled with punctures and were black and blue from wrists to shoulders. Brenda's nurses were overworked and the pressures of constant attention to many children had worked against Brenda's special need for fluids. Brenda became worse and was near death.

It was at this point that Brenda's mother asked for a special nurse. The doctor felt that this was not necessary but agreed only to make the parents happy. The nurse in this instance was Brenda's aunt. It immediately became obvious that this was a good move, for the special nurse gave Brenda special attention and had her drinking from a cup almost immediately after her arrival. Brenda recovered quickly.

There are times when a special nurse is definitely necessary as in Brenda's case, regardless of the views of either doctors or nurses to the contrary.

The minister of seven-year-old Ivy came into her hospital room loaded down with toys. Ivy was thrilled, but her nurse was not. The scissors were too pointed. The crayons were toxic if chewed upon. The eyes of the teddy bear were easily removable and could accidentally be swallowed. The doll had arrived in a thin, plastic bag that could smother a child who placed it over her head. Painting in a hospital bed is quite messy. The nurse also confiscated the half-melted chocolates and the crumbling cookies.

It is difficult to know just what to bring a child who is hospitalized. Food should never be brought without the nurse's approval. Small children appreciate a favorite cuddly toy from home. Three-year-old girls always like dolls, and boys enjoy objects with large and safe movable parts. A favorite toy of three-year-old Peter was a plastic chicken that laid an egg whenever he pressed it to his mattress. Peter was amused and thrilled every time the egg emerged, and he played the game over and over.

Games offering manual therapy are best. Coloring books with nontoxic crayons, silly putty which does not mess the bed, magic slates, puzzles with large wooden pieces, kaleidoscopes, and magnets are all gifts that offer endless variation.

Teenagers appreciate puzzles that are worked with their hands. The square plastic puzzle holding smaller squares that are moved about into various combinations of either numbers or comic figures is a toy that offers endless amusement. Most hospitalized teenagers enjoy light reading contained in small magazines which are easier to pick up and put down than books.

Returning Home

Five-year-old Evan upon returning home from the hospital awoke nightly, screaming from nightmares. His parents were in a quandary as to the cause.

Two-year-old Darlene seemed to cry for no reason whenever she was laid in her bed. Her parents wondered what was the matter.

Evan's parents finally got him to talk about his nightmares. Evan thought he had been placed in the hospital for being bad. His dream involved a bad action on his part and immediately he was sent to the hospital for punishment. His parents finally assured him that this was not the case and Evan's nightmares ceased.

Darlene's parents finally found that her screaming coincided with the appearance of anything white. The white sheets reminded her of the hospital and she screamed to be taken from them. A white dress worn by her mother sent her into a tantrum, and even her father's white shirt repulsed her. The white sources of displeasure were removed for two weeks and Darlene returned to normal.

Many children upon returning home need constant reassurance of their parents' love. Four-year-old Charles insisted that his father sleep with him every night for a week. Three-year-old Alice could not sleep unless her mother held her hand.

Many parents agree that a good deal of conversation and explanations are necessary upon a child's return home. Others feel that explanation should also occur *before* a child goes into the hospital. Joy's parents went to the library and got a book about hospitals and read it to her hoping that this might help if she ever was admitted.

Some books which may help children to understand hospital experiences are these:

Julia Ann Bartok, *Kenny Visits the Hospital* (Jericho, N.Y.: Exposition Press, 1956).

Florence W. Rowland, *Let's Go to a Hospital* (New York: G. P. Putnam's Sons, 1968).

Josephine Abbot Sever, *Johnny Goes to the Hospital* (Boston: Houghton Mifflin, 1953).

Margaret Cosgrove, *Your Hospital: A Modern Miracle* (New York: Dodd, Mead & Co., 1962).

James L. Collier, *Danny Goes to the Hospital* (New York: Norton & Company, Inc., 1970).

Eleanor Kay, *Let's Find Out About the Hospital* (New York: Franklin Watts, 1971).

Alfons Weber, *Elizabeth Gets Well* (New York: Crowell, 1970).

Arthur Shay, *What Happens When You Go to the Hospital* (Chicago: Reilly and Lee, 1969).

Sara Bonnett Stein, *A Hospital Stay* (New York: Walker and Company, 1974).

Eleanor Kay, *The Clinic* (New York: Franklin Watts, 1971).

Eleanor Kay, *The Emergency Room* (New York: Franklin Watts, 1970).

Margaret & H. A. Ray, *Curious George Goes to the Hospital* (Boston: Houghton Mifflin, 1966).

Such books can help a child to adjust to a hospital experience. A visit to the hospital, if allowed, will also be beneficial.

10

Premarital Counseling

Many legislators are seriously thinking of passing laws which will make it more difficult to become married. To them it seems obvious that many persons are not ready for marriage when the wedding day arrives.

Ministers have long recognized the fact that some young people who come to them are not truly ready for marriage, but they also realize that if they do not marry them, someone else will. That someone else may be a justice of the peace, judge, or minister not of the faith of the couple involved. It would be better for the couple to be married by someone of their faith who can begin to establish a healthy relationship with them.

Young people, who know their minister as a friend, will find premarital counseling more meaningful and will involve themselves more deeply with less anxiety.

Whether those involved are friends or not, the minister should feel a responsibility to offer some type of premarital counseling to all who come to him and to begin to build a friendly, open, and honest relationship that will be helpful after marriage as well.

The first contact with the minister concerning marriage is usually a phone call by the woman. The minister immediately should make an appointment to see the woman and her fiance at a stated time of approximately one hour in duration and suggest seeing them both on at least two other occasions. *Three* interviews should be planned.

If the first interview is scheduled for more than one week away, the minister, if he is sure that this particular couple is ready for marriage, should send them the following material or its equivalent:

1. Three copies of a routine form, which can be mimeographed, with blanks to be filled in relative to full names, addresses, telephone numbers, date of wedding, time of wedding, place of wedding,

single or double ring ceremony, religion, honeymoon dates, marriage tests planned, and any other data the minister desires to know.

2. Two copies of the pamphlet: "Thinking About Marriage."
3. Two copies of "A Courtship Analysis."
4. Two copies of "Marriage Role Expectation Inventory."
5. Copy for the girl entitled: "Your Wedding Workbook."
6. Copy of the wedding ceremony.

(All of the pamphlets mentioned are available to ministers and counselors through Family Life Publications, 219 Henderson Street, Post Office Box 427, Saluda, North Carolina 28773.)

If the material listed above has not been mailed out to the couple prior to the first interview, it will be handed out at the close of the first session. (It should not be mailed out unless the minister is confident of the friendship with those involved.) Individuals and situations differ. It is particularly worth keeping in mind that some of this material for premarital counseling would not be appropriate for use with divorced persons. The approach in that case requires some different steps and it will be discussed later in the chapter.

Even when the couple knows the minister well, they may not wish to use this kind of material. When this happens the minister might be alerted to the possibility that this couple might not really be ready to face the basic responsibilities of marriage. While there are exceptions, those who are eager to learn as much as possible about their future marital relationship, will generally respond favorably to the use of materials like these. In some cases, they may even ask for more publications and request additional times for discussion.

The first interview often cements the relationships. It is an informal session in which the minister gets to know the couple better and explains the procedure.

A second interview will be directly related to the material handed out as listed above and can move into those areas of greatest interest to the couple. At the close of the second interview, the minister may request that the couple take the "Sex Knowledge Inventory" test released by Family Life Publications. This test should be given to those who would like to further their knowledge in this area by their own admission and to those the minister feels definitely are lacking in sex knowledge. The test takes one hour to complete and will necessitate another separate interview for discussion. Counselor's guides for all tests released by Family Life Publications are available to the minister, and the booklet, "A Doctor's Marital Guide" is also available and may be given to all couples.

During the second interview the marriage plans as such can be discussed briefly, but the detailed discussion of the ceremony itself is left for the third and final interview.

The minister who finds difficulty in establishing an alliance with couples may find it helpful to use a brief mimeographed yes or no questionnaire and to have the couple score themselves.

An example of such a questionnaire follows:

ARE YOU READY FOR MARRIAGE?

	YES	NO
1. Do you believe that the marriage ceremony is a solemn promise to live together until death do you part?	___	___
2. Do you share common interests in religion, education, and outside activities?	___	___
3. Do you have all the necessary sex data?	___	___
4. Do you know your mate's faults?	___	___
5. Can you afford a down payment on a house?	___	___
6. Can you afford a two weeks honeymoon without financial worries?	___	___
7. Does HIS occupation offer security now and in the future and is HER occupation compatible with family plans?	___	___
8. Have you known each other for more than one year?	___	___
9. Can you talk together openly and honestly about ANYTHING?	___	___
10. Can you both forget past arguments and jealousies without further discussion?	___	___

Score ten points for each YES
90–100 Wed tomorrow
70–80 Wait awhile
50–60 Flirting with divorce
Below 50—Not for you.

This questionnaire serves as an icebreaker and often stimulates quite a response from the intellectually oriented who will start a good discussion by saying, "You can't answer some of these questions yes or no." You need only reply, "Which ones, and why not?" and the interview will progress quite interestingly.

It is a well known fact that many young men will not plan their honeymoon. They just assume that when the wedding is over they will take off for Niagara Falls or elsewhere and all will end happily ever after. Every young groom should be strongly urged to plan that first night! He should discuss the sexual aspect, the place, his approach.

No minister has lived up to his or her responsibility who has not broached this subject directly with the man. Too often the whole marriage begins dreadfully for lack of planning on the part of the groom, and young brides call home or church in tears and occasionally hysteria. Brides are exhausted after a wedding and the groom should make every effort to plan well the first few days of the honeymoon. As the questionnaire indicates, two weeks is suggested.

IN SUMMARY. The minister should plan at least *three* interviews of one-hour duration separated by days as time allows. The interviews to follow a thought-out pattern:

1. Interview to establish rapport and to distribute forms, pamphlets, books.
2. Interview to discuss forms and materials distributed.
3. Interview to establish details of wedding.

Every minister should establish an individual pattern of interviews and number of interviews, but it is best to be realistic. Planning too many sessions will often lead to frustration and cancelled appointments. Whatever your procedure make it known to your congregation. Good premarital counseling may lead to good marriage counseling and to better marriages.

THE WEDDING CEREMONY

BASIC PROCEDURES. Couples have for a long time taken an active role in designing and choosing parts of the wedding ceremony. Recent years, however, have seen this an even greater preference on the part of men and women to become personally involved in formulating the plans. The wise minister will recognize that this interest promises to hold many valuable opportunities for discussions about the meaning of marriage. He or she can helpfully refer the couple to a variety of useful resources, traditions, and plans. As these alternatives are discussed, the meaning and theological significance can be explored and the couple may find in both traditional and innovative ideas some very meaningful ways to express their faith in God and their commitment to one another.

For those who prefer a familiar approach, the following procedures provide a basic design that may be altered in a variety of ways.

When the couple is ready, it is helpful to give them a copy of the standard wedding ceremony. Some ministers put a diagram of the ceremony on the back of the sheet. At this point, even the couples who have indicated a preference for the more traditional style may have an opportunity to suggest modifications.

If the wedding is to be relatively small, a rehearsal is not necessary.

In this case, the couple and the wedding party meet the minister in the study for a half hour before the service in order that explicit instructions can be given and questions answered.

Larger weddings generally require a rehearsal. It should be held at a mutually satisfactory time for all concerned, usually the night before the wedding. During the rehearsal, the head usher or "director" plays an important part. When a head usher is used, his responsibilities include seating the guests, lining up the participants, and cuing the organist. The procedure which he is to follow is usually worked out quite carefully before the rehearsal begins. He should, however, be sure to give attention to the entrance and exit. They are often the most difficult parts of the service. He should also request photographers not to take pictures during the ceremony. If pictures in the church are wanted, the wedding party may return to the front of the church after the ceremony, when all the guests have left. When a director is used, many of the same procedures should be followed. The director is often a friend of the family who is knowledgeable about the procedures and who has a knack for guiding people to be in the right place at the right time.

The couple is usually responsible for choosing the music and for obtaining an organist. If requested to do so, the minister may contact the church organist. It is helpful if the church has determined a set of guidelines for these and other matters involved in the use of the church. In this case, the church guidelines may suggest an honorarium for the organist, which is not usually less than twenty dollars. The flowers should be ordered by the bride in accord with the church guidelines, and the arrangements for delivering the flowers should be made in advance.

If janitorial services are needed, the minister should refer the couple to the church custodian and indicate the fee designated in the guidelines of the church for this arrangement.

Generally, there is no set "fee" for the minister. This is usually handled in a variety of ways, at the discretion of the minister. Couples who can afford to do so, should consider an honorarium of not less than twenty-five dollars. If the minister must drive any distance, the travel expenses should be repaid with mileage reimbursed at the rate of twenty cents per mile.

THE WEDDING REHEARSAL

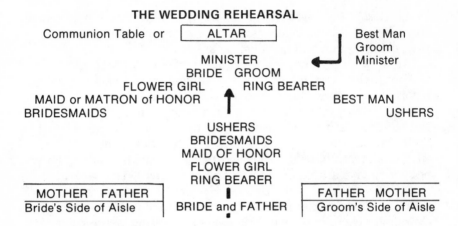

1. Everyone be seated. (Look over diagram carefully.)
2. Take your places at the rear of the church aisle. The best man will hold the ring for the bride's finger, and the maid of honor will hold the ring to be placed on groom's finger.
3. The organ will be playing (prelude) while the head usher seats the bride's mother (pretend), then the head usher will tell the organist: "The bride's mother is seated and the bride and her party are *all* here." The organist will play for *three* minutes approximately, and then play the *wedding* march.
4. If there is a carpet to be rolled down the aisle, or back up the aisle as it is stacked in front, then it will be done so after the mother is seated and during the three minutes noted above.
5. When the wedding march begins, the groom, the best man, and the minister will enter through door at right of the sanctuary and face down the aisle toward the procession from places as shown.
6. When the bride reaches the front pew, the groom will step forward and give her his left arm as they turn to face the minister. The father stands to the side and one step behind the bride until he gives her in marriage. When the minister says, "Who gives this woman to be married to this man?" the father says, "I do," and then sits next to his wife. If no father is living, then a close male relative may stand in.
7. ALL take places as indicated in diagram above.
8. Procession down aisle begins on LEFT foot, bring right toe to the left heel, then step forward with right foot, and bring left toe to right heel. Two arms length between marchers.
9. When all are in position, the organist will stop, and the minister will read over the words which call for responses and repeats.
10. After a prayer, the minister, at the request of the couple may say, "You may kiss the bride," and after the kiss, the participants will go out in reverse order with the bride and groom first.
11. Ushers will return and usher out one aisle at a time, beginning with the bride's parents at the front aisle. Ushers should arrive one half hour before service begins and help in any way they can.

Two Special Concerns

There are at least two cases when special care is needed. One of these occurs when the prospective bride is pregnant. Such a circumstance calls for tact and sympathy on the part of the minister. It is generally a time when considerable anxiety is felt by everyone.

If it is known that the young woman is pregnant, then the minister should discuss the matter with her alone, then with the father of the child, and then with the parents involved. On many occasions after calm discussion it can be concluded that the girl should go to a home for unwed mothers, deliver the child, and then decide if she still wishes to marry, or to give the child up for adoption and start over again. The nine-month period can be a time of testing the boy involved to see if he is going to assume mature responsibility by working, saving money, preparing a place to live for his family, and maintaining a close tie with the girl. Most homes for unwed mothers will at the same time counsel the young woman and man. If a girl decides not to marry and desires an abortion, more counseling is advised. It is not unrealistic to involve others who can provide medical or legal help at this point. At least six additional hours can be useful in talking through the relevant issues.

The second case involving special attention occurs when one or both of the partners have been married before. Although premarital counseling is just as important, the questions asked by the minister will differ greatly, and such persons will be more reluctant, as a rule, to answer them. It is often easier to counsel those who have been married before separately on two occasions, and together on the third occasion.

Many ministers have noticed that one divorce leads to two and that people frequently choose new mates who have the same faults as their previous mates. Often they will choose a partner with the same faults to a greater degree! Thus, it is important for the divorced person thinking of marriage to be aware of the patterns of a former mate, and of one's own marital patterns.

The minister counseling divorced persons who wish to marry again will have to establish a rapport in the first interview, avoiding at all times being judgmental, and then ask relevant questions on the second interview. Such questions are designed to bring all the objectivity possible to bear on the future marriage relationship and will be helpful if counseling continues after marriage.

The questions asked of divorced persons in the second interview should be directive in nature, while the first interview was non-directive in nature. Why do you feel your first marriage failed? If it was your partner's fault, do you take any blame at all? What activities did you share with your first mate, and what activities will you share with your new husband or wife?

TEN GUIDELINES FOR SECOND MARRIAGES

In the 1960s it was reported that there were 300,000 more marriages a year than in the previous decade and approximately half of those were remarriages.

More and more ministers and churches are going to have to be more knowledgeable, tolerant, and program-wise in dealing with the problems of divorce and remarriage.

1. Divorced persons should not rush into remarriage quickly. They should first rid themselves of passive hostility and resentment that can poison a second marriage. All thoughts of revenge should be overcome. This takes at least a year and preferably 18 months.

2. Those who remarry should know that *money* is a real problem. It now holds a top place in causes of marital conflict. All monetary plans should be discussed in detail before remarriage as well as after.

3. Be flexible in handling the children of your new mate. Do not demand or expect love and obedience. Be open, honest, courteous, and let the relationship evolve slowly. Discretion is the better part of valor. Allow your new mate to cooperate with the first wife or husband in dealing with the children. You are now "one" in all relationships but this.

4. Do not move into an apartment that either of you lived in with a former mate. There are too many associations and memories.

5. Be flexible in your sex relationship. Endeavor to approach sex in new ways that you have never tried before. If you always had sex in the bedroom, lights out, attempt to move the scene with the lights on, etc. Mates who have already experienced diverse sex will need a new approach both physically and psychically.

6. Skepticism and cynicism will be apparent in regard to life, love, and marriage. Do not force the issue as if in a court of law. Acceptance, reassurance, and steady display of affection will soon turn the tide. Positive thinking helps.

7. Strive not to be defensive or sensitive to criticism. Hold yourself in high regard and never think of yourself as a substitute for the former mate. You are a unique being with your own worth; know that worth!

8. Believe that your mate does love you even though his or her way of showing it may differ from that of your first spouse. Doubt may come occasionally, but do not dwell on it.

9. Do not resent discussion about the other mate. Learn all you can and use it to your benefit. When you have heard it all announce the end to the discussion. Here again, a year and a half may be needed. Do not criticize the other's first spouse. If you see the second marriage disintegrating, do not give up without six months of marriage counseling.

10. Marriage is hard work and takes blood, sweat, and tears. Work at it.

11

When Life Ceases

When death comes the minister goes. Of all the problems and events in human experience religion plays the primary role in the adventure of death. No other source of help is available. There is nowhere else to turn. One's personal faith may occasionally suffice for the nonchurch member, but this too is a religious orientation. Funeral directors have served to lighten the burden in a practical and necessary way, but they alone can never fill the need of the bereaved.

When death comes, the church and the minister embody a religious faith that is immediately available. At the first notice that death has come the minister responds immediately regardless of time or circumstance.

Upon arriving at the home, sympathy and heartfelt concern is given. This is *not* the time to preach a sermon. There will often be many things the bereaved will wish to say. Some things will be said over and over. Words are of little consequence. If a faith has not been built by the parishioner before death it is no time to start in the midst of present tragedy. The minister's concern is the primary factor and his or her *presence* alone can indicate such a concern. We are too often embarrassed by silence, forgetting that silence is often an opportunity for meditation.

The eternal question, "Why?" will surely arise. Here again, no sermon is in order. To enter into profound theological explanation serves only as an extremely frustrating experience. It would suffice to say, "The ways of God are difficult to understand." The most important factor in religion is God. The minister must assert this faith simply and indicate that if we have faith in God we shall fear nothing. If our parishioner at this point lacks faith in God it is understandable and *words* at this point will avail naught. The minister stands for this unshakable faith. Further, the minister is the emissary of a church that stands for this faith in God in the midst of all suffering and sorrow. This symbolic inference speaks for itself in a time when words come hard. The first call is a call of real concern. It should be brief, unless the bereaved has a great deal of guilt and emotion to unburden. In this case, sympathetic listening is therapeutic and religious in its effect.

On the following day after the initial call the pastor will make an appointment for a second call for the explicit purpose of discussing the funeral service. The following factors are essential:

Day and time of service
Place service will be held
Place of burial
Type of service desired
Open or closed casket
Cremation and subsequent committal

Other details will be worked out by the funeral director and often all of them will be. Churches which have a tradition of insisting that the service be in the church and which have a set order of service and procedures are fortunate in the sense that everyone involved knows just what to expect.

If there is no set service, it would be well for the minister to draw up a list of "suggested" procedures for consideration. At the time of death it is too late for such objectivity.

After the funeral service is over the minister should pause briefly to speak to the closest relative of the bereaved and make a tentative appointment for the next pastoral call—generally the day following the funeral and not later than three days after. This call will show continued concern. It will follow the general rule in pastoral calling of accepting persons where they are and then leading them to higher ground. It is at this point that religious faith can be explored together in a more direct manner as necessary and without anxiety. If emotional tension is still high, if God is cursed or denied, sympathy and understanding will still be the best religious response. The pastor's faith in God will assert itself gently and without doubt, without sermonizing. In fact, such preaching is often influenced by the minister's own doubts, and he finds, upon inspection, that he is preaching to *himself*. The parishioner must "feel" the faith, not hear it. The minister's constant concern and stability suffice.

As the days pass, the rebuilding of stronger faith occurs, not because the minister verbally gives it, but because he encourages it by care and love.

THE DEATH OF AN INFANT

There has been very little written about ministerial procedure at the time of the death of a baby at birth or shortly after birth.

Quite often the young parents are stunned. The mother often becomes hysterical and weeps for days. The father is so upset at the grief of his wife he does not know what to do. Often the mother has had to undergo surgery for an unnatural birth and is not only mentally depressed but physically in a dangerous condition. The husband has only one thought and that is mainly for the well-being of his wife.

It is at this point that the hospital authorities ask him, "What are you going to do about the dead baby?" Having never given this a thought the young man is in a complete quandary. The hospital superintendent is often insistent to the point of rudeness. "Who is your undertaker going to be?" At this point thoughts rush in . . . an *undertaker* . . . a *funeral* . . . *expenses* . . . *cemetery lot* and *burial* . . . *minister*.

It is my hope that he calls his *minister* immediately. The minister should be well prepared for such a call and should move very *slowly* and with great discretion.

The steps that follow are these:

1. Arrange to talk with the husband alone (after the usual brief sympathy call on the wife).

2. Give him the name of an undertaker who is sympathetic with the feelings of parents at such a time.

3. Explain that the undertaker will keep the child until a decision is made for a funeral service.

4. Discuss with the husband the following:

   a) *Naming the child* Often the baby born dead is not named. Some prefer that a name be given and that the stillborn child be symbolically "named" at the time of his committal. Even though the child was born dead it must be remembered that he was a "living" person to the mother who carried him. The naming of the child must be discussed with the wife. Quite often the name chosen by them in the early months is set aside if it was a family name so that a relative will not be disappointed, and a name is given that the couple would not wish to use on the next child to be born.

   b) *The ambivalent feelings involved* In most cases the parents feel somewhat responsible for the death. The mother mentions her lack of rest, her activities, her smoking or drinking, her neglect of her doctor's orders, etc. The father sometimes confesses he did not want the child because his family was large enough already. Such feelings should be discussed when the parents are so inclined.

c) *Accepting the wife's grief as normal* Most men cannot tolerate the misery and weeping of their wives. Their tendency is often to lash out at God, the nurse, or even the minister. The minister should explain that the wife should display the normal grief reactions, the weeping is often common with mothers who have healthy babies due to the relief of anxiety and the tension of waiting to deliver. Our religion does not help us to avoid grief but to live *through* it, to accept it.

5. After discussing these points the minister and the husband are ready to talk to the wife (often two days later).

6. The minister goes first, let us say, at 2:30 and the husband follows at 3:00. The minister discusses the same three points with the wife (a, b, c).

7. The husband enters the hospital room, the child is named, the funeral arrangements discussed. The time of the service is set by the three present. (The minister should have knowledge of *times* that are convenient for the undertaker and thus know of no conflict.)

8. The minister gives a copy of the service to the wife and suggests that she read the service to herself at the time the infant is to be buried. If the child is to be christened, dedicated, or baptized, the mother should also have the certificate in her hands before the service.

9. The service takes place at the *grave*, in accordance with the funeral practices of the denomination. Usually only the immediate family is present, and often only the minister, father, and undertaker.

10. The minister continues usual pastoral duties and the necessary non-directive counseling.

In summary, the minister should be prepared for the death of the infant for he will often be called upon to guide the entire path of the young couple. This guidance should not be rushed but should move *slowly* with great sympathy and sensitivity.

12

The Church Secretary Brings Efficiency to Church Life

A good church secretary is a bridge between the minister and the congregation. She adds a dimension of goodwill in an area of the business administration of the church.

In this chapter the word, "she" will be used, but we are all aware that a male secretary may be preferred by some ministers, or that other members of the staff or congregation often do "secretarial" work.

TELEPHONING

The phone rings often in a busy church and the secretary should be instructed to answer it cheerfully. "First Church, Miss Jones speaking." It is my feeling that church calls are often personal in nature and the secretary should not ask, "Who may I say is calling." If callers wish to leave names and messages it is entirely their decision. Some parishioners will wish to talk with the secretary, and she should be a warm listener but never give advice when problems of a personal nature are discussed. Such problems should be noted on her pad for the minister. If the caller is deeply troubled the secretary should be able to say when the minister can be reached or will call back.

There are occasions when the minister will ask the secretary to call parishioners to inquire whether or not they need a pastoral call. In this regard the minister will give a date book marking open areas when such calls can be made.

Calling parishioners to remind them of important meetings is vital on many occasions. Such a call should be warm and the data given with a concern for the feedback given. Church members should not feel that they are being prodded into attending a meeting but rather only being cheerfully notified of the event.

The minister who wants to stay on top of things will sometimes choose to have a second phone installed in his residence with the same number as that of the church office. Whenever the secretary is not on duty and the minister is working at home, the phone may be answered there.

PARISHIONER FILES

A file on every church member should be updated. One box card file is sufficient with names, addresses, members of the family, ages, and past and present church duties.

The mailing list should always be updated and available to church leaders who wish to do their own calling. If addressograph plates are used the tabs should be colored with coded references. For example, all yellow tabs are members of the Couples Club; all red tabs are members of the Governing Board, etc. When a member serves on more than one committee there will be different colors on the tabs. This way volunteers can easily pick out addressograph plates for special mailings to special groups.

The mailing list and the files should fall under three headings: Members, Friends, Potential. We all have peripheral parishioners, and we all have some people who can be considered potential parishioners. The secretary should keep them on the mailing list and call them once a year to see if they wish to continue to receive church mailings. The list of Friends and Potential should be handed out to the Membership Committee so that they may greet, call, seek them out, invite them to attend church or functions with them.

The secretary is responsible for files on all members. She should record and tell the minister the names of all persons who sign the church register or pew Welcome cards. She should record all births, deaths, weddings, and baptisms. She should keep a file on shut-ins for use of calling committees or groups wishing to serve them.

TYPING AND MIMEOGRAPHING

If the church has a set order of service, the minister needs only jot in the hymns, readings, and responsive readings, etc. for the Sunday morning bulletin. He or she should jot these notes on a mimeographed form and on the back of the form make notes for the Sunday bulletin announcements. The order of service should be prepared for use by choir director before choir rehearsals.

The church newsletter should be edited by a church member. The printing and typing may be done by the secretary, but volunteers should be actively involved in the news. Newsletter policy should be set by the governing board or minister. Church newsletters should not be used for carrying on battles between personalities.

The secretary should type neat form letters and positively keep a copy of letters sent out, especially by the minister. She should take notes at all meetings which are included in her responsibilities and send them out to members of the group or committee. Tape recordings and typing of sermons should be done as requested, but the minister may wish to edit before final printing. Learning to use office machinery may take some time and ministers should be patient. Addresses of people who repair machines should be in the secretary's files.

COMMITTEE LIAISON AND REPORTER

When advisable the secretary should attend meetings as requested by the minister or group leader. She should be able to find any files and data needed for the conduct of specific meetings.

She may be asked to instruct the janitor as to the setting up of chairs, tables, and other accessories for a good setting for the meeting. She should be a good hostess at governing board meetings and aid in the preparation of refreshments and serving as needed.

When the minister cannot attend a meeting he may instruct the secretary to take notes and report to him. She should make this known to the committee or group and ask for their permission to do so. When the minister is out of the office for long periods, a specific time of each day should be set aside for the secretary to call the minister and report. This time may be one half hour before or after the minister's usual dinner time in the evening.

The secretary should know when to interrupt the minister's day off and when to protect him from interruption on the day off. In this regard the secretary has to be perceptive enough to learn to know what is an emergency and what is not or when information is vital to the minister's job and when it is not. This all takes time as each gets to know the other.

CONFIDANTE

A good secretary knows how to speak clearly on the phone, listen to a parishioner talk in his or her office, and keep all personal matters confidential. The rule of confidentiality that applies in the medical field also applies in the religious realm.

As a receptionist, she may hear a great deal of confidential outpouring and listen non-directively, without judgment or advice, and calmly assure the parishioner that the minister can help and will be glad to respond as soon as he is free to do so.

She should know the minister's schedule and know when to make an appointment for a troubled person. For example, the minister might tell the secretary that he or she is keeping Tuesday evenings open from six to eleven and that she may freely schedule any person in need of help or counsel and write it into his or her desk calendar.

A good secretary puts the minister first and not the church. This is one good reason for never hiring a church member as a minister's secretary. A nonchurch member will tend to be more objective. In hiring a secretary, only a mature person should be considered. The best age would be near forty, when all children are well along in school and up to age sixty, depending on vigorous health. She should always be discreet.

WORK HOURS

The work hours will depend upon the salary allowed, the work hours of the minister, and the size of the congregation. Assuming the minister spends each week day in his office from nine A.M. to noon, then he might only have a secretary work in the afternoons. The secretary would be on duty all day when the minister takes his day off. She would report in to him at a set time on that day if necessary. Depending on the monthly meetings the minister wishes her to attend in the evening, hours would be arranged.

The church secretary may be on a stand-by basis on Sunday mornings or during worship service. In this sense she would pick up any loose ends necessary before and after the services, and during coffee hours or similar gatherings.

In a typical church of approximately five hundred members the secretary might work on the following schedule.

MONDAY   9–12; 1–5   Recall Sunday events, needs, telephoning, etc.

TUESDAY   9–5 Minister's day off
WEDNESDAY   1–5 (Correspondence, files)
THURSDAY   9–4 (Sunday bulletins, mimeographing, typing)

FRIDAY   off
SATURDAY   off
SUNDAY   9–1 Miscellaneous jobs (if Sunday employment
                    is deemed appropriate by both minister
                    and secretary).

This approximates a thirty hour week, yet, like the minister, five to ten hours a week more would be added as occasion arises.

This schedule assumes the minister will be in his office on Monday, Wednesday, and Friday mornings. For constant phone coverage, minister or secretary may have the same phone number of the church installed in their home and use a jack system to share coverage.

TEN RULES FOR SECRETARIAL SURVIVAL

1. Never criticize the boss unless he asks for it.
2. Never take sides in a church debate.
3. Never play amateur psychiatrist with the parishioners.
4. Never be indiscreet in dress and manner.
5. Keep stated office hours religiously.
6. Do not misplace your trust.
7. Never accept a resignation from church duties of any member yourself.
8. With difficult parishioners use the same rule we apply with children, "be firm but gentle."
9. Have a job outline that the governing board of the church approves and knows full well.
10. Smile.

SOME OBSERVATIONS

Any curiosity about the personal life of the secretary should be related to whether or not that life-style will interfere with the total ministry of the church.

An open honesty about health both of minister and secretary should be disclosed as confidential information. Because of health factors one or the other may do a certain amount of work at home.

Some days will be much busier than others. If the secretary sees that overtime will be necessary and she has a previous engagement she should say so as soon as possible so that her boss can plan the work schedule.

The secretary's relationship to her minister's spouse is something that should be thoroughly discussed. A church secretary is not responsible for doing jobs for the minister's spouse, nor is she responsible for reporting every move the minister makes. Discretion is important here. The secretary must be firm but gentle in dealing with her boss's mate.

Every church secretary should know the "chain of command" in the church, especially when the minister is away. Who she should call in regard to issues or problems should be outlined on a chart by use of squares and lines as in any other organization.

It is advisable to hold weekly sessions with the minister and secretary talking about job outlines, expectations, compensations, and goals. These sessions should not take much more than one hour a week. They will help solidify the relationship in a businesslike way. This is not a parent-child relationship, no mothering or fathering. There must be professional distance and yet a deep and warm respect.

13

Keeping Cool
When Under Fire

There is a story about a clergyman in a small community who would leave town every day at five o'clock. He was so consistent in his exodus that the local gossips became curious. After months had passed, a parishioner finally found the courage to ask the preacher where he went every day at five o'clock. The young minister responded, "At the end of every day I get into my car and drive down to the railroad tracks and wait. Then at ten minutes past five the train goes by. I sigh, and say to myself, 'Thank heaven there goes something I don't have to push!' "

A congregation of church members cannot be pushed, but they can be led. A minister cannot direct the sheep but can guide them. No minister can command respect; it must be earned. Often it is the church leaders who help make a minister a good minister.

The mistakes of the clergy that cause reluctant parishioners and balking trustees and tension between shepherd and sheep are commonly made during the first year of the new pastorate. These first year mistakes include:

1. Spending all of one's time on administration to the neglect of pastoral calling.

2. Neglecting the elderly members to favor young people.

3. Making radical changes in the traditional service of worship.

4. Preaching on controversial political issues.

5. Becoming involved in a controversy with the organist or choir director.

6. Misplacing one's trust by appointing the wrong people to do important church work.

7. Listening to advice given by the wrong people.

8. Betraying confidences.

9. Neglecting stated church office hours where one can be reached consistently.

10. Encouraging radical programs with the teen-agers.

11. Assuming that some parishioner is "against" him or her.

12. Criticizing members who lag behind the church program from the pulpit or in the newsletter.

Many of the above errors could be avoided if pastors upon entering a new parish would keep their minds on *one* goal only: the establishment of a strong bond of friendship with every member *before* pushing policy decisions in any area of parish administration. Each individual church member must feel that the minister truly cares. This process of building strong personal ties takes calls, and calls, and more calls in the first year. Such face-to-face confrontation builds a situation of mutual trust and concern. When such fellowship exists, the minister will be trusted to lead, to guide, to be a "decision maker." He or she shall have earned respect, and his or her advice will be sought after.

In the ministry, the title and office alone do not assure the allegiance of the congregation. The parable of "The Lost Sheep" is significant, and the pastor must truly love every single member of the congregation. They will respond with life.

Criticism

Anyone who does anything, says anything, or stands for anything will be criticized. Criticism is inevitable in the ministry for all ministers do something, say something, and stand for something.

The minister will often be criticized by those who *do nothing* and *stand for nothing* but say plenty. The criticism of the neurotic must be ignored, yet as a person this individual should receive our prayers and empathy.

But what of the criticism of those who are good members of our churches?

I recall a man converted from an orthodox religion who entered the service of worship just as my sermon began. He seated himself in the front pew, took out pad and pencil and proceeded to write his weekly critique of my morning message. The sum of his criticism was mailed to me weekly. For four years his criticism was acknowledged and the giver thanked. The key here was *acceptance*.

Dear Parishioner:
    I received your note and appreciate your concern for my ministry and our church.

                                          Sincerely yours,

                                          Pastor

When the minister is criticized as not having done the work, an inventory must be taken. If the minister has fulfilled pastoral obligations, then he or she should save personal defense for the governing body of the church. It is good discipline to take notes on daily activity: calls made, meetings attended, hours worked per week, etc., and to give a written report each month to the governing boards.

If you prepared a job outline as suggested in Chapter 1, in cooperation with your lay leaders, it will be easy for you to defend yourself with support from those leaders.

The general attitude will often be, "My gosh, he or she is really working too hard."

TEN RULES TO FOLLOW WHEN UNDER FIRE

1. Always call upon your critic at the first sign of discontent if an active church member.
2. Never accept a resignation from persons who feel they have been hurt, unless you want them to resign. Always show them they are needed, if they truly are.
3. Never write critical letters in answer to a critic's letter.
4. Use the telephone often to keep in touch with your critics after the initial blow-up, on a bi-weekly basis. Critics often crave extra attention.
5. Always go forth to say "hello" to a critic. Go out of your way to greet him cheerfully.
6. Always look for an unspoken cause of your critic's anger. There may be marital problems or work problems and they are being taken out in frustration on you and your position.
7. Remember that whenever you feel disliked, most often the other person feels that you dislike him or her.
8. Most critics have a personality clash with you. Try to understand what it is in your personality or in that of the other individual that causes the clash.
9. Keep in close touch with the friends of your critics.
10. Accept criticism as inevitable in your work and refuse to become depressed.

TEN RULES FOR STAYING ALIVE

1. NEVER HAVE MORE THAN ONE FACTION IN YOUR CHURCH ANGRY AT YOU AT THE SAME TIME.
   Every church has its divisions by AGES and by other classification, i.e., "Liberals," "Conservatives," and "Middle-of-the-roaders." Make your own classifications to fit your particular church.
2. DEVELOP A PROGRAM TO COVER ALL AGES AND INTERESTS.
   A Sunday school is primary; have youth groups and adult groups for social purposes and serious purposes; and have as many committees as necessary (open meetings).

3. BUILD STRONG FRIENDSHIPS THROUGH PASTORAL CALLING.

   Make an average of nine calls a week, and use the *telephone* often.

4. BE CERTAIN OF THE LOYALTY OF A VAST MAJORITY OF YOUR MEMBERS BEFORE MAKING ANY DRAMATIC CHANGES.

   It takes approximately one year and a half, preferably three years, to build loyalty enough to alter worship forms or traditions. Otherwise you will face unforgettable resentment.

5. HOLD STATED OFFICE HOURS AND BE THERE.

   This type of consistency will impress the business person and make you available in time of need. Have a phone in your home with the same number as your church study.

6. PRIOR TO IMPORTANT MEETINGS, MEET WITH YOUR LEADERS.

   You may make an appointment in their office, or yours, or over lunch to discuss details of the upcoming meeting.

7. TAKE CRITICISM NON-DIRECTIVELY, AND THEN MAKE ANOTHER APPOINTMENT WITH YOUR CRITIC A FEW DAYS LATER.

   Do not accept resignations without discussing it later or they will come back to haunt you.

8. NEITHER BETRAY A TRUST OR MISPLACE YOUR TRUST.

   We fall into the trap of discussing members at their insistence and prying, and we too readily place new members in high positions.

9. TAKE ONE FULL DAY OFF A WEEK WITHOUT FAIL.

   Death and near death are exceptions. You must retain physical health and family ties.

10. MEDITATE, READ, FILE, BROOD BEGINNING ON MONDAY AND THEN WRITE OUT THE SERMON ON SATURDAY MORNING.

    Picking a sermon topic in advance is half the battle. Make notes during the week and you will write more easily. Rest on Saturday afternoon, get physical exercise, and never go out on Saturday nights.

14
Personal Faith and Self Reliance

From early colonial days until approximately twenty years ago the clergy held a unique position in the community. They were respected and revered for their sensitivity and their knowledge. They were admired for their quiet virtue as well as their righteous indignation. They were set above the crowd and yet there was no "gap" between them and their people.

Today the clergy strive feverishly to stand in the world with their people and the "gap" begins to grow wider and wider. Seemingly this is a paradox and yet it appears that the closer a minister becomes to the people in the pews the further the minister stands from them. Let me give you some examples.

I watched a young minister waltz among the people at a church conference bedecked in a sensational pea green jacket. He was trying to be like the young people present, yet he was not really accepted by them.

I watched a minister move through a conference in his turtle neck shirt without tie. He was trying to be one with the forty-year-old business executives present, but somehow he did not fit in.

I read a newsletter from a minister who had just taken a new pulpit and in it she wrote: "I do not make calls. My task is similar to that of a doctor. You must call me for an appointment." I watched the gap widen in that woman's church between her and her elderly members.

I watched a minister with beard and ducktail allow draft dodgers to use his church for sanctuary but even with those to whom he gave that sanctuary he did not seem to have any rapport.

I watched a female minister drink champagne at a wedding reception, and for a moment I thought she might have narrowed the gap, but later in the evening the people with whom she was conversing went off to another corner and criticized the way the young minister held her glass.

We talk often of dialogue but we fail to communicate with the average church member because we no longer take a unique position based upon our clerical ground. We continue to strive to follow the crowd, hoping to meet our people where they are, when we should be leading them to where they ought to be, and they expect this of us. We know the church must move into the world but we must move the church into the world while we are in some sense aspiring to that kingdom which is beyond the world: the kingdom of peace and brotherhood.

We are of this world but we must not forget, as our people have not forgotten, that we also part of another world.

Sometime ago, Pastor Jones was called on the carpet by the Chairman of the Board of Trustees. He was told that he was hired and he should follow orders!

The Chairman wanted the Pastor to sing three hymns instead of two, put the responsive reading after the prayer, and take the offering after the sermon. He asked Pastor Jones to change his Youth Program, and to stop preaching against divorce. (The Chairman had been divorced.)

Should Pastor Jones follow orders?

Is a minister hired or called?

Traditionally a minister is called to serve a church, just as a doctor is called by a sick patient. When the doctor arrives the patient does not presume to tell the doctor what to prescribe. He or she calls the doctor, who has been trained in a particular profession, and takes the advice of the doctor.

Nearly all of today's ministers have had seven years of college training plus actual experience in the field. Are they to forget it all and follow orders often thoughtlessly given by someone who wants to be boss?

It is frequently said that *every* member of the congregation is the minister's boss. This is a poor choice of words. A good minister is a servant, not an employee; a shepherd, not a sheep or a goat. He or she doesn't follow, but leads. He or she doesn't preach what someone else believes, but preaches what *he* or *she* believes. He or she doesn't vacillate as the wind blows and as a trustee directs, but has his or her point of view.

A minister is not hired; he or she is called.

In the past we led people into paths of righteousness, now we follow them into paths of foolishness and the gap widens. We have been unwitting pawns of rightists and leftists, socialists and fascists, demonstrators and racists, when we should have maintained an individual stance relative to our own unique religious concerns.

In the past we were often other worldly, striving for a kingdom not yet fully known and paradoxically, there was no gap. Now we are often as secular in outlook as others, striving for goals of this world, and yet the gap between minister and congregation is growing wider. We must be in the world and yet not of the world.

Most religions in America have been losing ground. People are attending church less, giving less, joining in diminishing numbers relative to population growth. The more the church moves into the world, the further from the world it becomes, and the gap widens.

To close the gap, ministers must once again lead public opinion and not follow it! We must lead toward our respective religious goals. We must define our role by our speech and action. We must paint the picture of the kingdom clearly and indicate that we are now part of that kingdom in word and deed. We must make it clear that we are allied with that which is beyond the here and now and that we are related to that which is infinite and eternal. As ministers we are "not of this world," yet we are working within this world.

People everywhere are looking for religious leadership. The people of this nation still look for prophetic voices, still seek strength from the church, but the church seems to be looking for strength from the people. When the church loses its way and loses its own unique religious role then it will surely die and the clergy will blame the people while the people will blame the clergy.

The more we become one with our people the more we will see a gap because our people do not expect us to be just one of the crowd. They expect us to be just a little better than the crowd, or at least to represent that which is beyond the earthly, and when we fail to represent that which is the other then we lose our place in society as clergy.

How can we close the gap?

How can we move the church into the world and yet still be "not of this world"?

We must stand first of all as clergy, and secondly we must stand as individuals who speak from a religious position of personal integrity.

Once we accept the fact that we are ordained ministers, ordained to speak on all issues from a religious position it will be easier for us to move our church into the world.

We should speak out as individuals who through personal meditation have something to say. We should not join any secular group or movement; we should LEAD our own church and not follow secular opinion.

Jesus was not a member of any vocal sect, he spoke from the dictates of his own conscience. He led the disciples; he did not follow them.

Martin Luther King, Jr. seldom mentioned his affiliation with the NAACP or any religious sect. He was a member of a sect but he preached from his own *personal* convictions. He did not follow his people; he led them. Albert Schweitzer only rarely mentioned any affiliation to any sect; he developed his own faith and chose his own personal course of action. He was often criticized by the medical profession to which he belonged, but he paid no attention to them and practiced medicine according to his own concepts, according to his personal meditation and religious insight. Schweitzer avowed that God spoke to him daily to carry on his work.

Gandhi seldom mentioned any affiliation to a religious sect. He followed the dictates of his own conscience through personal meditation. He often asserted that anyone who did not take religion into politics didn't know what religion was.

The key is this: we must discover how to move the church into the world and yet at the same time relate words and actions to RELIGIOUS insight at every step.

The clergy of our time must speak from their own *personal* convictions whenever they hope to lead the church into the world. They should not follow the views of sect or caucus, of right or left, or any other group that tries to push them. Whenever they wish to enter the political arena they must do a great deal of meditating in order to base their action on their personal religious convictions with integrity and courage. Only in this way does the church move into the world as it encourages each individual member to follow the example of religious leadership and to do their own thing from their own religious convictions.

When the minister moves into the world on his or her own religious conviction he or she will be fulfilling his or her role and he or she will find the respect of people who will strive to follow an example and there will be no gap between them because everyone will know just where he or she stands.

Ministers should not follow any party line. They can only follow personal convictions, and if they have no convictions based on religious faith then they should leave the ministry.

Times like ours demand people with the courage of their convictions. This is what our people expect of us and this is what our God expects of us. Move the church into the world from your own religious faith in your own personal way and your church will come alive again.